For Jan,

May the tools and resources
in this book elevate and
expand the love in your
relationships beyond all that
you have ever known.

Love & Peace

i

The Relationship Toolbox

Resources to expand and elevate your experience of love.

The Relationship Tool Box

Resources to expand and elevate your experience of love

© 2018 Kenneth H. Brixey, Jr.

Dedication

This book is dedicated to Cathy - my friend, my confidant, my sounding board, my greatest supporter and my wife... just to name a few.

The inspiration for this work is the amazing blessing that this relationship with Cathy has been for close to twenty-five years of marriage and nearly a year of dating before that. It has been absolutely wonderful. I am so grateful to have a relationship that even after all this time, I find reasons and inspiration daily to see our relationship with awe and gratitude of how it has grown and expanded. I am inspired each day to do my part in keeping the relationship growing and elevating.

Cathy makes it easy; she is loving even when she has every reason not to be, and she is almost blind to my faults. To be a better partner, all I need do is follow her lead.

Thank you, Cathy; I love you deeply.

Heartfelt Gratitude

My deepest gratitude and heartfelt appreciation go out to Kim Green, partner and Art Director at **Short Story Marketing**, for the beautiful book cover design of this book. When you are ready to design your logo, book cover, website, marketing material and much more, Short Story Marketing is an invaluable asset in creating the perfect look for you, your work and your company.

www.shortstorymarketing.com

I also am so very grateful to my editor. While she asks to remain anonymous, I must acknowledge her here.

You have been instrumental in the process of readying this book for publication. The journey to completion has been so much easier with your assistance and knowledge. Your countless hours of correcting my grammatical errors and your suggestions on phrasing, allowed me the freedom to focus more fully on the content presented here.

Even though I will honor your wishes, and not mention your name, I pray you know how much I appreciate and treasure your contribution to this work.

I sincerely and lovingly thank you both.

Insights into the relationship that inspired this book

During these twenty-five plus years that my wife, Cathy, and I have traveled together, we have never had an argument or fight of any kind. Now there are folks out there, even some so-called experts, who will tell you that it is healthy to fight; that fighting adds a spark to a relationship. To believe that arguing and fighting is healthy is an illusion, and I suggest you test the theory for yourself by giving the tools in this book a chance.

Sure, there is energy created from the argument. The fear, the anger, the sadness, the pain, the raw emotion all add up to negative energy that needs to be released. When we find that release and those beautiful emotions of love and joy rush in and replace negativity, the passion that is created makes the experience seem extraordinary and even beneficial.

I say, why fight? Why go through the negative just to get to the positive? Why create chaos just to find peace? Instead, find a way to clear the air, then put your energy toward expanding the love and joy. Create meaningful love and emotion instead of the chaos and fear, and you will create a passion filled relationship. Cathy and I choose not to have the negative side of things; and yes, it is a choice we still make every day. We still express our differences of opinion; we just find ways to release the negativity without the need for fighting. We choose to seek understanding and joy over the fighting and heartache that comes with the chaos. We have happily decided it is okay to disagree and have our own opinions.

It is possible to have the euphoric emotions of passionate love without the conflict. You can have the love without the fight. You can have the happiness without the sadness. Just as a dark room will never be lit with more darkness, love will never expand and elevate with anything other than more love.

I am not here to convince you that fighting is bad. Sometimes fighting, if handled in a healthy way, is an option for some folks to get their deepest feelings out. For some folks, the anger is the only way they know to express an opinion or stand their ground. If you are one of those, I suggest learning new ways; there really are very calm and peaceful ways to express your feelings without the fighting. If you must fight, do so in a way that you do no harm; do not harm others or self in the process.

A common theme throughout this book is this: no judgments allowed. I am not here to judge, and I ask you to remove judgment from your relationship and even your life. Judgment is the predecessor to anger, fear and those not so wonderful fights. This book is here to offer new thinking, new ideas, and new possibility. When you give these methods, considerations, suggestions and tools a chance, you will certainly find ways that will work to assist you in elevating the love and peace in your relationship.

Since we are all unique individuals, there will be no one way that is right for all relationships. This book will offer some tips, practices, and even some sacred rituals that have proven successful in many relationships as well as my own. Use them as a starting point. If they work, use them, if they don't work, don't use them. However, if the action you take does not work, look at it. Is there some part of the action where you withheld love? Is there some part of it where you did not give it your all? Is there any part of it that you can take and use to create something unique for you and your partner?

Oh, by the way, many people have a very legitimate sounding excuse for not trying to make the relationship work anymore. They say that their partner will never participate in any of the practices, tools and sacred rituals presented here. I am here to tell you that most of these will work to transform your relationship even if you are the only one participating. The change you feel may be your perception of things and that is a perfect place to start. A shift in perception opens us to see more of that which we wish to see. The shift you experience may be a realization that things are not as bad as you thought and that is wonderful. It may be that you realize it is time to make some changes in your relationship and that too is very powerful knowledge that can lead you to a very healthy relationship; and you may realize that the relationship you have given up on may be salvageable and perfect for you. You may also discover that the relationship you heal is the one you have with yourself.

When I tell you that I am going to offer some ideas that have proven successful, I do not speak of this lightly. My relationship is an extremely important part of my life just as it is for many people. I pay attention to what is working and what is not working, and so does my wife. We work together. We put the time in to make this successful.

Most of us put in time and effort to make our career a success. Some of us have hobbies that we dedicate much effort and time towards. Those of you with children put in vast amounts of time to make sure the kids are well and provided for. We must do the same for our intimate relationships. A relationship does not automatically go down the road you hope it will travel all by itself. It does not stay the perfect Utopia you find in the dating period without some guidance, some effort, some dedication and continuous expansion of awareness. A relationship grows and changes and shifts just as the people in the relationship grow and change and shift. To have a relationship that works as you and your partner grow and evolve requires you to tune in; tune into your partner; tune into you; tune into the relationship. Without awareness, adjustment, evolution and growth, your relationship becomes stagnant. Relationships take awareness; they take work and guidance and visioning and intention setting.

So here is an insight into the relationship that inspired this book:

Cathy and I always make sure love and happiness are our priorities, and we never go to bed upset with one another which is easy since we do not let an upset stay around for very long no matter what time of day it may occur. Even the upsets are rare in our relationship. We do not always see eye to eye, and we make it okay to not agree. Because we truly work together and care about each other's happiness, we usually come to some agreement, and I can only think of a handful of times we could not agree. In nearly every situation, we find a solution that outweighs the disconnect an argument will cause. In those rare times we could not come to an immediate agreement, we either tabled the topic long enough to consider the other's point of view, or we found a way for one of us to be okay with the fact that the other was doing something we did not fully agree with. If we could not come to agreement or compromise, we shifted our focus completely; we did not ignore the topic, we just allowed love to be more important.

To simplify, we do not allow the relationship to become damaged by our need to force our point or for an ill-conceived need to be right. On the rare occasion that we find ourselves at an impasse with no solution in sight, we simply chose love, peace and happiness. The relationship always remains our top priority and that is more important than getting our way in everything.

We both do our parts to compromise, concede an opinion and anything else we need to keep the relationship strong. You know the most incredible thing about that? In all the years of practicing this agreement in our relationship, I do not feel that I have missed a thing. I have never felt that I gave up my since of self, my authenticity. In fact, I feel just the opposite. I feel that I have only gained through this whole experience. I have grown, and I have learned more about being the person I need to be to sustain, elevate and expand me, Cathy and our relationship.

Before you begin believing we live in the Magic Kingdom or that we live with a really different set of circumstances that allow this peaceful union to occur, let me assure you we live with the same circumstances and in the same world as many other relationships. In fact, we had, and in some cases still have, a tremendous number of hurdles piled in front of us just like many people face. I will even go so far as to venture out on a limb here and say there are some things we face each day that many people do not. I will not venture any further down that road as comparing serves no one. Since all circumstances and people are different, there really is no way to accurately compare, anyway.

More than once, Cathy and I have faced one of the biggest reasons marriages fail and ultimately end; financial problems. There were days we had no clue how we were going to keep a roof over our heads. There were days that car trouble threatened to prevent us from making it to work. There were days that a trip to the grocery store was questionable. Needless to say, it has not all been peaches and crème in the financial department.

Also, many couples do not do well when they spend too much time together. Of the twenty-five plus years we have been together, Cathy and I have worked side by side for more than seventeen of those years. To make matters more difficult, I was her boss for some of that, and she was my boss for some of it. She and I were even co-owners of three companies which we ran simultaneously. I saw things being run from an operational standpoint while her style was more of a bottom-line financial standpoint. While this could have been a source of disagreement, we chose instead, to allow our different viewpoints to work together to create a powerful partnership.

Even in the hectic work environment, love was our main focus. The secondary focus was customer service and providing the greatest experience possible for clients and employees. Even though we saw different ways of attaining our goals, we remained focused on what we both desired.

During the times we did not work together, one or both of us were in jobs that demanded extremely long hours away from each other. I held a job for a while that had me on the road from several weeks at a time up to two months straight without coming home. So, you can see, we have run the extremes of that pendulum. We swung from being together 24-7 for years all the way to being physically distant for months at a time, as well.

We have both had two other marriages, which obviously did not work out the way we thought they would. There is a lot of baggage associated with that as well. So, no, we do not have magical powers or live a sheltered life. We proved that we could not only survive what many people consider difficult marriages; we could thrive and continue elevating and expanding our relationship. We are examples that problems and difficult times can be faced together and instead of the circumstances destroying the relationship, a new and unique relationship can be formed. Any relationship can be transformed into one that works when intention and desire are the focus.

What we have above all is the desire to figure it all out and make it work. We basically un-learned everything we thought we knew about relationships and created a life together that works for us. We did not throw away our experiences from the past relationships, we adjusted and learned and re-created. We created tools and resources as we went along and still create new ones today.

I would like to say that our success is because I am a saint to live with and that I acted like her Prince Charming every moment of every day. I would like to say that, but I cannot do so without bending the truth a bit. While she truly is an angel, (just ask anybody who knows her), the success we have realized in our relationship is due to continuous practice of the tools presented throughout this book, and we maintain our focus on love.

We both worked to succeed in our relationship each and every day, and we still do. We do not wait until something goes wrong before we pull out the Relationship toolbox. It is always out, always open, and we do not hesitate to pull out a tool; not to use on the other, but to use for ourselves and the relationship. Our way of working on the relationship reminds me of a wonderful quote by Zig Ziglar as he responded to a remark from a member of his audience about motivation not lasting… "You say motivation doesn't last. Well neither does a bath. That is why we recommend one daily."

Relationships are not one commitment or positive action then you are done; they are the culmination of compassionate time together, consistent commitment to each other and the relationship. A successful relationship is growing constantly, and most of all, using love as a verb. Using love as a verb is giving loving energy to everything you do within the relationship for yourself and your partner.

Using these tools is not a chore. It does take a little work and at first it is a little difficult to create the habit, but it truly does become a natural behavior and can even be fun. Being aware of your behaviors in the relationship and having a desire to change is your first step. After that it really is an enjoyable exchange. You trade a behavior that does not empower the relationship for a tool that will enhance your life together; therefore, you empower your relationship, your partner and yourself. To me, I enjoy getting to know Cathy at least a little more each day. She is ever evolving; just as you and everyone you know. I learn more each day, just as she does with me. We do not see change as a bad thing, but one of new adventure, new pathways and new life. I love being able to surprise her still and keep things fresh. I do this by being fully committed to her and the relationship. I do this by keeping my awareness of her and the relationship open and understanding. I do this by putting love first; just as she does for our relationship and me.

Now, don't think this is all just a way to keep her happy. Well, it is that, but it also makes me extremely happy to please her and to grow our life together. It makes life much more enjoyable to have a partner that likes being with me. It is amazing to have someone I look forward to seeing even if we have only been apart for a short while, and it is just as awesome to have someone look forward to seeing me. Life without tension and anger in the home is beautiful. So yes, I am a little selfish in all this as well.

Like I said earlier, this is not a magic potion. It is simply the use of some tools that are proven to work. These tools must be used in order for them to be beneficial to you. Just as the tools you have in your shed must be pulled down off the shelve and used before they can do any good, these relationship tools must be pulled out, dusted off and put to use before you will experience growth in your relationship.

Cathy is the reason I learned these tools. Because of her, I have an incredible collection of empowering relationship tips to present to you. Enjoy and start now in building your Amazing and Authentic Relationships!

Table of Contents

Opening Awareness
Seeing the Truth of Your Relationship

Start Where You Are
Notice What is Working

Elevate and Expand Your Relationship
Create New Behaviors and Expressions of Love

Create Sacred Rituals
Elevate and Expand Your Experience of Love

Introduction

Did you know that the only way possible to experience any part of this human existence is through relationships? You have relationships with people, places, things and situations; every instant of your existence is within a relationship. To some extent, you are in relationship with every person on this planet, everything ever created. You are in a relationship with your higher power whether you believe that to be God, Allah, Universe, Highest Self, Source or anything larger than you, and of course, you are in a very intimate relationship with yourself. Every awareness that enters your experience is due to your relationship with that thing, that situation, or that person. Relationships are complex series of reactions and/or responses to someone or something. Sometimes the reaction or response is fleeting, here one moment and gone the next. Sometimes it can be a life-long experience. Sometimes the relationship is a surface level experience with little emotion surrounding it, and in other times it can be deeply meaningful, good or bad and carry much impact into your life. Sometimes it is full of joy, and other times it may be a negative experience.

You cannot separate yourself from relationships. Even if you wanted to end all relationships with the people you know, it is impossible. Sure, you can move to a cave in the middle of nowhere, seclude yourself from all exposure to human kind, leave your television, phone, radio, computer and any other communication device behind; however, you will still have relationships with people through memory, and those memories shape your experience. Even in that secluded cave, you will still have relationship with everything around you. Even in sensory deprivation tanks, you have relationship with the tank, the air you breathe, the feelings you experience and, of course, you will be in relationship with yourself.

Memories keep relationships alive. This is why you can still foster and grow and heal relationships with those people who have transitioned from this human experience or who have moved out of your life for some reason or another. Unless you have had some sort of total mind clearing experience where you have no recall or memory, you will be in relationship with people for as long as you live and beyond.

You are in relationship with the air you breathe, the water you drink, the sights and sounds in this world and so much more. For instance, the relationship you have with food determines your physical shape and plays a huge role in your health. Relationships are truly what mold the life you live. And, the way you perceive the relationship, the way you express in the relationship, the way you experience life because of the relationship is truly what matters in creating the life you desire. And, you get to choose your experience of everything. This is extremely good news, and you will see this truth as we move forward in this book.

You can perceive and express in any way you choose in relationships. You can perceive every relationship positively or negatively. It truly is a choice. You choose your relationship experiences just as you choose your life. In fact, the way you choose to experience and perceive your relationships greatly determines how you experience life.

There are many relationships in your life that are happy and serve your highest good. These relationships can come in the form of people; your friends, family or intimate partners. They can come from your relationship on the spiritual level. They can also come from the relationship you have with your home, car, food or anything where you experience gratitude in your life.

Some people have relationships that are not so positive and maybe even abusive. You may have relationships with people that just do not work to bring you happiness or comfort; they may bring only pain and suffering. It may be a co-worker, family member, a current or ex-lover that appears to have created a gap between you and peace. It may be a car that is on its last leg or a home that you are about leave; these can all seem to create a negative vibe in your life that leads to chaos, upset, anger, sadness and, of course, the dreaded fear of change.

Many people find they have some relationships that are working very well while others are not. The relationships that are not working well can cast unease, chaos and fear into those relationships that would otherwise serve you well. For instance, you may have a great home and the relationship with this home is bringing you peace, security and comfort. On the other hand, the relationship with your partner may be a struggle and shadow the goodness of the relationship with your home.

In situations such as these, you can easily experience uneasiness throughout your life or as a dear friend of mine puts it, dis-ease. And yes, that play on the word is intended. Negative relationship can cast shadows over all relationships and each of your life experiences. This is especially evident in the work place. You may find your relationships with all but one of your co-workers to be in great places, but that one is difficult or disrupting, at best. This creates a feeling of worry lying wait just below the surface in all you do and casts all your work relationships into the shadow of fear for what may come.

When you realize the one negative relationship is casting its shadow over many others, you can turn your focus to those that are working. There is no greater feeling than the feeling you have while a relationship is working. Even when there is nothing extraordinary happening within the relationship, it seems that all is well in the world. When things are working in a relationship everything flows beautifully together, and it seems easy and effortless as you enjoy life. This is how life begins to feel when you are whole in the relationship with yourself.

From this loving place you find the resources and abilities to take all of your relationships to new levels that will most certainly serve your highest good. Life takes on new meaning and miracles seem to happen all around you. The sky is a little bluer and the breeze is a little more refreshing. Music carries a more magical sound and blends with life a little more melodically. Food even seems to taste better when all is well within your relationships and yourself.

While the tools mentioned in this book are designed to benefit romantic relationships, most of the tools will work for any relationship including your relationship with you. If you are not currently interested in romance, you will still find valuable information here, so stay engaged. I mention this here because we are about to move into the use of these tools in intimate and romantic situations and relationships.

How you experience your relationships extends beyond the walls of your heart and body. The energy found in a thriving relationship carries outside the perceived boundaries of the relationship. When you are in a positive and loving relationship, friends, co-workers and family can all feel a more loving vibration and sense a more glowing aura around you every time you enter the room. Daily tasks do not seem to be as tedious, and you look forward to being back with your partner as quickly as you can. Because you are in a much happier place, a higher vibration, your work, your connection to others and nearly every aspect of your life truly lifts to new noticeable levels. And you are not the only one who can feel this shift. Life really does take a step up.

Conversely, life can be a living hell when your relationship is not working. Each moment of the day can seem like an absolute struggle. Dread, sadness, depression, anger and other negativity towards the relationship become the emotions of your life when things take a dive into that dark vortex. Energy and vibrations take a hit, and it is felt as much as the higher vibrations of the working relationships.

Couples tend to go numb when the energy drops even if there is no discernible reason for the decrease. This is not necessarily as negative as most people think. When you feel that drop in energy and cannot find a reason, you are opening awareness to the energy within you, your partner or the relationship. This drop in energy is not an invitation to contribute to the negativity. It is a call to action; a call to healing.

If allowed to continue, the numbness that sets in becomes difficult, at best, to climb back out of and the relationship often goes into stagnation until someone finds the courage to take a step in one direction or the other. If you consider the divorce rates these days, you can easily see the direction most of those steps take.

Too often, couples rely on the special occasions to be the spark that reignites the romance in the relationship. Christmas, Valentine's Day, Birthdays and Anniversaries are

5

relied on to save many relationships. Unfortunately, those special occasions only come once a year each. So, if you keep count, there is Valentine's Day, Christmas (mentioned here due to the gift giving), New Years, Anniversary, Birthdays and maybe a couple of others. At best you may have five or six "Special Occasions" compared to the other three hundred sixty or so regular days. What ends up happening is that little thought to relationship growth is given on all those other days.

Sure, many of you may deliberate over picking the right gifts, finding the most romantic places for dinner or choosing the cards that say the perfect things to your significant other; that does add to the love and enhance the relationship. While all those things are great and sometimes even awesome, they are not what hold the relationship together. All too often the special occasions are expected to boost or save the relationship when these occasions serve only to recognize the relationship you have already been living all year long. The tendency is to go through the motions during rest of the year and this does not elevate and expand the relationship to higher levels. It is good to remember that the gifts, dinners and other things you do on those special days do not make the relationship; it is the daily actions and behaviors; the daily re-commitment and choice to elevate and expand the relationship that create the relationship you desire.

Keep in mind, a relationship is not a destination; it truly is an adventure, a journey; every single day. When you treat the relationship and your partner as a never ending journey of discovery, the awe and wonder of your journey together stay present. Curiosity in a relationship does not "kill the cat"; it creates opportunity for awakening to understanding. It creates chances for growth and excitement.

6

Never settle in the fact that you think you know all there is to know about your relationship or your partner. Your partner, your relationship and you are continuously evolving, and the newness is always there waiting for someone to uncover it and experience it. Think back to when you first fell in love, when you first met; there was newness and discovering that kept the spark ignited. Keep the search for new discoveries alive.

If you want to expand and elevate your relationship, the real work starts after those special occasions mentioned earlier. The real work happens each and every day of the year as you blend your lives together. The real work is not work if you are striving to grow your relationship. When you take the extra steps and keep discovery, excitement and newness alive, those special occasions become a way to celebrate how the relationship has grown over the past year and a way to recognize the accomplishments you and your partner made throughout the year. These special occasions are not intended to be a slingshot that makes things right enough to last for the upcoming year; they are stepping stones to create a momentum of growth and deeper understanding. These special occasions are opportunities to celebrate the growth you and your partner have achieved throughout the year.

This book introduces you to relationship tools that will help you take your relationship to the next level and beyond; each and every day. Whether your relationship is the best it has ever been or in serious trouble, you can move it to new and empowered levels; first by re-committing, by choosing to grow and then by taking a step.

We are funny creatures, we humans. We think that just because we made the decision at one point to be in a relationship, we need do nothing else. That decision is merely the first step. There are decisions to be made every single day, actions to be taken every day, words to be spoken every day, it is not hard, it just takes attention and intention to keep your relationship growing and thriving.

Most relationships can truly be exactly what we dream; however, some are not. Many people may actually be in a relationship right now that is truly over. You may be hanging on due to guilt about "failing" and what it will look like to you and the people around you if the relationship ends. You may be holding out hope that a miracle will come along and save the relationship. You may simply not want to face the ensuing battle that in your mind is inevitable. The battle in your mind does not have to take place. The obstacles we see before us in most all of life's journeys are much more horrible in our imagination than the truth of what they are; merely hiccups in our path.

Even if the relationship is as horrible as you think it is, it can still elevate and expand. It does not have to remain hateful and angry, it can become loving and caring even as it comes to an end. There is enough hate and anger in this world for many more lifetimes. Why add to it by dissolving a relationship on bad terms? There is something about your partner that you like, if not love very much or the hesitation to walk away would not be so strong. There are ways to find that again and use it to start your new life without the bitterness, anger, depression and sadness of a sour breakup.

Many of the relationship tools you are about to read will assist you in empowering you while finding healthy ways to begin anew. You will also find ways to create beautiful and strong foundations for your life which can be beneficial to any relationship you enter into in the future.

Now, for the single folks out there, before you tune out thinking this book is not for you, you too are in relationships. You may not be in a romantic one at this time, but you are in relationships every time you encounter someone. Most importantly, you are in a relationship with yourself. Read on and you will benefit from most of these tools as well.

The relationship you have with yourself is often hard to handle for many. As hard as you may try not to be, you are affected by your own actions, thoughts and feelings more than any other person can affect you. You are in constant conversations with yourself. Some of you do it out loud and others are quieter about it, but everyone does it. You are literally in an incredibly intimate relationship with you so each of these tools can be used to more fully understand yourself, as well. In doing so, you create a space where you can be more authentic and present with yourself as well as your relationships with others.

Before moving into our Relationship Tool Box let's talk about what a relationship with another person is for a minute. A relationship is truly a blend of two people. When your relationship is healthy you are not in it to be changed or to change someone else. You serve the relationship and your partner best when you are authentically you and allow them to be authentically them. To change, as an attempt to make someone else happy, cheats you, them and the relationship. And to attempt to change them cheats everyone as well. To blend is to remain the unique individual that you are while allowing your partner to do the same. When the two people blend, beauty and love rise to new levels; growth of the individuals and of the relationship is welcome and elevates the entire experience. When blending happens, both parties become stronger and complement each other's strengths.

I have heard from many people and even read this on different social media sites, "A relationship is 50/50." This could not be further from the true. An authentic and healthy relationship is 100/100, a divorce is 50/50, if you are lucky enough to have everything split down the middle. A relationship requires you to give one hundred percent of you while joyfully allowing your partner to give one hundred percent of them. This is not a competition and everyone's one hundred percent is different. We will talk more about one hundred percent and its importance later in the book.

One of the foundations of a relationship is trust; the problem though is often, trust is given a warped definition. Sure, it is nice to be able to trust your partner and it is okay to hold some expectation of trust. However, all too often, trust gets thrown around and used as some sort of a weapon of mass destruction for the relationship.

Many people call a trust foul; every time they get their feelings hurt or things don't go their way. When their partner says something or looks at them a certain way, they come to believe that their partner has broken trust and can no longer be counted on for support or love. Some people call a trust foul every time they think their partner does something wrong, whether the partner actually does something wrong or not. All it takes for this to happen in some relationships is a thought of something bad to pop up that seems even remotely possible and all of a sudden, the partner cannot be trusted. A person will think about the possibility of their partner cheating and insecurities, self-doubt, feelings of not good enough come rushing in and build an instant wall between the partner and the person who thought the illusion. Mistrust explodes into full-fledged epidemic proportions if allowed a chance to exist. Seek first to trust yourself and trust your partner to be the person they have always been.

Trust really is important in the relationship, however, put your focus on love first. Remain focused on the love you are sending out above all things. Anytime you focus on something else, especially a negative thing or a sense of lack in some area of the relationship, you are detracting from the love you send and you will only draw in more of the negative things and more lack into your relationship.

When you share love, love elevates and expands; when you withhold love, love decreases within you, within the relationship and eventually within your partner. Trust in the power of love and your trust will be placed right where it needs to be in order to empower the relationship.

Once you begin to doubt your partner and find yourself in that place where you feel trust has been depleted your mind can play some amazing tricks on you. It becomes extremely easy to begin making stuff up, which we will talk more about later, and paranoia sets in.

If paranoia and making stuff up is allowed to fester, look out because "get them before they get you" behaviors are soon to follow. Stop those poisonous thoughts and beliefs in their tracks. "Get them before they get you" behavior serves no one and can easily cause more destruction in the relationship than the act, or perceived act, which began this train of thought in the first place. This behavior has damaged and ended more relationships than can be counted and leads to pain and suffering in your life, your partner's life, your friends' and family member's' lives; it just is an abominable snow ball of negativity that grows and grows as it rolls through your life. And to add to the turmoil and destruction that happens in the relationship, these beliefs and behaviors begin showing up in other areas of your life as well; work, family, friends, the cashier at the grocery store...

The next warning that deserves to be mentioned here is similar to "get them before they get you." Something may have truly happened in the relationship that hurt deeply. A common practice in this world today is to strike back. To hurt them as much or more than you were hurt. This is revenge and the results hurt everyone. No matter how deeply you got hurt; revenge serves no purpose and only adds to the pain.

There may be a very slight chance that you will feel better by taking revenge, but it will last only for a brief moment. Chances are if you are in touch with your heart at all, revenge will bring you nothing other than more pain. Revenge serves no purpose other than to drive a cold hard feeling deep into your soul that will take you much work to remove. After that you have to deal with self-forgiveness and don't we all have enough of that to do already?

Remember, if a behavior feels bad, don't do it. If someone could get hurt from an action you think of taking; stop and rethink it. Do not allow yourself to "fly off the handle" and react without thinking. Take a breath, check in with your feelings towards your next action and do what feels good to you, not what will hurt your partner the most. I promise, it will come back to haunt you even if only in your memories.

While there are many negative behaviors that could be discussed here, I want to mention only one more before we turn this around to the positive ways you can grow, rejuvenate, save, develop your relationship or in some cases lovingly bring the relationship to a close.

The last behavior I will mention here is pride. Pride can lead to any one or all of these negative behaviors and many more. Pride can shut down communication and create an atmosphere that is confining and restricts the growth you and your partner could have together. Pride leads to closing yourself off from learning because it tells you that you already know all you need to know.

Pride is often propped up by fear in an effort to create the illusion that someone is more confident than they really are. Pride is the projection that all is well despite the inner turmoil that may exist just below the surface. Pride has caused many relationship endings and will continue to do so when it is allowed to exist.

There are times you may feel you have done something that warrants a feeling of pride, feel it... for about 30 seconds then replace pride with gratitude. There is much more to come on the topic of gratitude later in this book.

Now, to hold you over until we talk more about gratitude try this quick and easy exercise. Think of one thing you have done in your relationship that gives you pride. Say out loud, "I am proud of myself for_____. Go ahead, say it out loud and feel the feelings associated with it. These feelings may really be positive and uplifting right now. That is perfectly fine. Go ahead and feel them and do not discount what you accomplished or how you feel.

Now, replace pride with gratitude. Repeat the statement and this time replace the word proud with the word grateful. "I am grateful for_____. Now tune into your feelings and the shift that takes place. Gratitude works on so many more levels than pride. It comes from that authenticity held within your heart instead of the ego-based thought system that runs on fear and negativity. Gratitude is something that stands on its own while pride needs the approval of others to hold any merit. Replace pride with gratitude in all you do, relationships, work, skills, creativity and everything else in your life.

As we move into these tools I ask that you read them, consider them and then give them a try. Take your time and gift yourself the opportunity to mindfully explore different tools and open your awareness to the results that you experience with each one. In this instant gratification society that we have created, the tendency is to jump in before we are ready and then expect huge results immediately. Relationships take time; they take patience; they take consideration.

Taking time to enhance a relationship is some of the sweetest joy you can have. It is not in having the perfect relationship that matters as much as the journey of building the perfect relationship. The journey is where the experience is found. Like you and me, the relationship is constantly expanding and growing. That growth and expansion will never cease as long as someone is feeding it and embracing it and honoring it with love.

As you read through these tools, consider how you can create a relationship enhancement practice. Honor you, honor your partner and honor your relationship by giving attention, intention, time and above all love to the journey of building an amazing union.

Okay, let's break out the relationship tools.

Opening Awareness

Seeing the truth of your relationship.

Opening Awareness

Only when we open awareness to our authentic selves will we see what is true, what is real and present. When we open awareness to our life situations without judgements or comparisons, we see the truth of everything in life. When we open awareness to truth, we see the foundation; the rock upon which we can build or re-build anything.

This especially holds true in relationships. When we open our awareness, we open ourselves to see and understand the foundation of the relationship. Every relationship has a foundation. The foundation is simply the base upon which the relationship is built, that solid place where once began our journey into relationship with our partner. Just as it is in construction, the more solid the foundation, the more stable the structure, or in this case, the relationship.

We can easily overlook the truth of our relationship and become blind to the foundation upon which it is built. We become entangled in things that we perceive as wrong and seek ways to "fix" them instead of holding fast to the foundation of love and joy that began the journey with our partner. We fall into judgment, blame, comparison or any `number of other things that we have learned over the years and hope the answers we seek, the healing we desire, can be found in fixing our partner or repairing the problems. One of the tools we will introduce later in the book is "Fix Nothing; Transform Everything." We can only do this when we are open to what is working and release our focus on what is not working.

The foundation of a relationship can be built of many things. Most relationship foundations begin with love and an attraction, physical, emotional or spiritual, to someone else. Many relationships begin with a foundation based on a physical attraction that has been perceived as love.

A foundation includes many of these and much more. A foundation can be strengthened by similar likes such as travel, books, food, music, and movies. Gardening, boating, exercise and other hobbies can be a major ingredient to a strong foundation, as well. The love of nature, festivals or even workshops can expand and empower the foundation. Sometimes the foundation may include similar spiritual beliefs. One of the most common things people consider to be part of a strong foundations is a sexual attraction for one another. Of course, these are all just examples and the foundation in your relationship may have different ingredients. The healthiest of relationships are built on foundations comprised of many common interests or the appreciation of each other's interests. Some foundations may even be strengthened when each individual hold similar dislikes about something.

No matter how many ingredients are present in the foundation, the key ingredient is love. A relationship will not grow and expand without love for each other as the main ingredient. We easily get caught up in the external things we have in common and rely on those things to keep our relationship solid. If for instance, you and your partner have the love of bicycling in common and build a relationship with this as a connecting action, all is well as long as you can bike together.

What happens if one of you injures a leg and is unable to ever bike again? If that is the glue holding the relationship together, the relationship is in for some rough roads on the journey to everlasting love. Same goes for travel, books, music and so on. If a love for books fades from one of you and not from the other, what is left? If love is the cornerstone of your foundation, then chances are good that you will find some way to overcome the gap that has formed in your levels of book love or bike rides or anything else you previously enjoyed together.

Opening awareness allows you to identify the true foundation of your relationship. There may not be a tangible commonality for you to identify like the books, movies and music mentioned before. Your foundation could be primarily the feelings you have for each other. If this is it, then this is perfect as well. Whatever the foundation is, though, this book will assist you to identify it and then look deeper. This journey will assist you to expand your awareness of the love that exists and then elevate It further than ever before.

If you are one of the fortunate ones experiencing a successful and loving relationship, the foundation may be quite obvious. You may not have to look very hard to identify the things that hold your relationship strong. However, even dysfunctional relationships have a foundation too. In these relationships the foundation may be an unhealthy behavior. Drugs, alcohol, physical and mental abuse, workaholism. Many other unhealthy behaviors and traits can serve to hold a relationship together, as well.

If you believe yourself to be in one of these dysfunctional relationships, this journey will assist you to find or create a healthy foundation. Awareness, desire and commitment become a powerful combination in manifesting anything you desire; even relationships.

Identifying the foundation, whether healthy or not, whether working or not-working, will allow you to have solid understanding and knowing. This understanding and knowing allow you to adjust your focus to something that will last, love. It will allow you to make sure that the foundation upon which you are building your life together is one of positivity and support instead of negativity and destruction. Knowing your foundation is one of love allows you to overcome any struggles that may arise.

One of the most important keys to identifying your foundation though is to look at your own relationship without comparing it to others. We will get into comparison later so for now, just leave comparison out of the equation. You and your partner and your relationship are perfectly unique and there is no other like it. Comparison is impossible, so just do not do it. You will save yourself a lot of heartache and turmoil and worry and stress.

Just as you are leaving comparison out of your relationship also leave out judgment. Do not judge your relationship as good or bad; see it as working or not working. Some relationships have a very unstable foundation, but they still have one. Allowing this foundation to continue the way it has always been, at the very least, brings you the same results or issues you have always had. If the relationship works for you like it is, perfect. Keep growing, elevating and expanding. If you struggle each day to keep the relationship upright on this unstable foundation, choose to make some changes that allow you to grow, elevate and expand as well.

The good news is that the foundation of your relationship is strengthened and expanded by simply tuning into it. Become aware of the foundation, good or bad, working or not-working, and move forward from there. If the foundation of your relationship is unstable, it is not an invitation to judge, criticize or destroy the relationship. It is simply an opportunity to make a shift, create a new foundation or strengthen the existing one. Tuning in and observing the relationship opens the door to make changes that allow the relationship to work for you and your partner. Simply notice if the foundation works or not, then adjust where needed. If a change you want to make works for you but not for your partner, consider a different change.

Ignoring the issues with the foundation of the relationship may seem easier at the time but it will lead to greater issues down the road and that road may not be very long. Addressing the issues when you discover them will be easier and put you and your partner on a positive and forward moving path much more quickly.

Like the foundation in your home, a little attention and TLC will mend the disrepair and maintain your foundation for years and years. Some need very little work and others may need major renovations. All can be strengthened and enhanced, and it all begins with awareness. Even the best foundations need attention all along the way, or they too can crumble and fail.

Any chance to improve or enhance your relationship relies on your willingness to reconnect with the foundation, fortify it and build upon it. How awesome would it be to carry your relationship further, stronger and steadier than ever before? The strength and health of the relationship's foundation is determined by the connection between you and your partner; the love you have for each other and the desire you have to grow, elevate and expand together.

To some, this all may seem a bit overwhelming and it may seem like a tremendous amount of work. The work required does not need to be difficult; it does not have to be work at all. The Relationship Tool Box is literally a collection of tools that, when used, empower, improve and elevate your relationship. These tools will open your awareness and will act as a guide to elevate and expand your relationship beyond your greatest desires. And, this journey can be fun when you choose to make it so.

Opening awareness requires willingness. You will be asked to look at your relationship and see all that is working to elevate and expand the love. You will be asked to look within to see what you may do to encourage the growth. You will be asked to look within and identify any behaviors that may exist that discourages growth or withholds love, as well.

Sometimes, the most powerful action you can practice in elevating your relationship, or anywhere else in life, is releasing that which no longer serves you, your partner or your relationship. And this is where we will begin.

Release What No Longer Serves

Relationships seem hard at times. Even the experts in the field of relationships tell you that it takes hard work, and some even tell you it takes sacrifice. I disagree that relationships must be hard, but I do agree there is a need for sacrifice. I believe you must sacrifice everything that does not express love, and you must sacrifice everything that does not infuse empowering energy. Since releasing what does not serve the relationship adds so many opportunities for elevating and expanding, how much of a sacrifice is it really?

Relationships do not have to be hard work; they simply need attention and intention. While that sometimes feels like work, it does not have to be hard. You can even make this work fun. Yes, it will be challenging at times; however, in challenges, doors are opened to something new. Facing the challenge with love and excitement and fun opens opportunities to create new ideas, understanding and desires that can elevate the relationship even further.

What gets in the way of believing these challenges and this work to be fun is the baggage carried into the relationship. Some of the baggage we carry is from previous relationships, some of it is what we have witnessed in the relationships of other couples, some of it comes from what we have seen on TV and in the movies. All of the baggage we carry, though, has been learned, and the good news about things we have learned, even the negative and destructive learning, is that we are capable of learning something new and different. What we have learned can be replaced or transformed with new learning, new beliefs and new behaviors.

The baggage we carry with us is demonstrated in many ways. While it may manifest in our lives and relationships through our different behaviors, all baggage primarily flows from one place, our thoughts. Our thoughts about what we experienced in previous or current relationships, thoughts about the relationships we see in the people around us; thoughts about the couples we see on TV and in the movies, all unite to create the baggage and beliefs we experience now.

Thoughts are powerful; they are energy and energy invites action - mental and physical. These thoughts become an emotional charge; emotional charge transform into beliefs; beliefs lead to action; action manifests into outcome, they create our reality.

This powerful sequence; thoughts - emotional charge – beliefs - actions – outcomes, can be an empowering journey in your relationship when it is based on positivity and love. It can also be a very destructive process if based on fear.

By the way, everything is perceived and acted upon from either love or fear, and you have the power to decide which is allowed in your life and your relationship.
Awareness of this sequence, beginning with your thoughts, is where you will realize empowerment. By opening awareness to your thoughts, you more fully understand, and ultimately control, your emotional charge, your beliefs, your actions and, of course, your outcome.

With understanding and awareness comes the ability to choose what you want and desire; you give yourself the opportunity to make empowering change throughout your life and relationship. You no longer need to remain stuck in

24

old patterns and behaviors that serve only to create pain and misery. You can see the value of what you think, believe, and do, and you can more clearly see the outcome before you.

Anything that does not serve to empower the love in your relationship must be changed if you want to elevate and expand your relationship. Most people see change as hard, something to dread; we see change as painful. To change, you step into vulnerability and this seems scary and overwhelming in many cases. The fear-based feelings create the assumption that change is hard; therefore, relationships seem hard. The saying, "Change happens only when the pain of staying the same outweighs the pain of changing," is often the truth.

Making a change, often seems hard, but it does not have to be. Change does not require pain. By opening awareness, you realize that most of the change needed in any part of your life and relationship is the simple act of release. Letting go of what no longer serves your relationship makes room for deeper love, appreciation and friendship. When the energy used to continue the negative behaviors, thoughts and beliefs is replaced with an energy that supports expanded love and kindness, relationships blossom into the beautiful experience they are meant to be.

Letting go; releasing something that has been a part of your "normal" for a while, even if that normal is harmful, feels like you are giving up a part of you. When you see this as giving up, it is easy to feel as if you have failed at making something work. You fail only when you continue doing the same thing over and over and expect different results. This is actually the definition of "insanity", but we won't go there at this point.

Sometimes the thing you need to release is woven into the very fabric of all that you believe a relationship to be. Sometimes the thing you need to release worked for you at some point, but no longer serves any purpose. Since it worked before, it is easy to believe it will work again so you hang on tightly. This does not serve you or your relationship.

When you can open your awareness to all that you think, believe or practice, you will see that which no longer serves the greater good for you or your relationship. Continue the things that benefit you and your relationship. Release that which no longer serves.

The tools presented in this first section of The Relationship Toolbox, point out some of the behaviors that do not serve in elevating relationships. In fact, the presence of these behaviors not only fail to serve your relationship, they can easily lead to the collapse of the relationship. Even if you and your partner manage to stay together while practicing these behaviors, your opportunity to elevate the love and strength in your relationship is limited at best.

Open your awareness to the thoughts and practices you have and release all that does not serve you, your partner and your relationship. An easy practice to assist in opening your awareness right now is to ask yourself questions.

> ➢   What am I thinking now?
> ➢   What value does this thought, or practice have?
> ➢   Does this thought, or behavior, serve the empowerment and growth of me, my partner, my relationship?

Do not judge your answers, just become more aware of what your thoughts and behaviors are doing for you. Are they serving the highest good of you, your partner and your relationship? In letting go of what does not serve, you, your partner and your relationships will heal and grow.

Leave Your Judgements at the Curb

One of the greatest gifts we have ever been given was given to us before we were born into this human experience. We were born with the ability to perceive all of life through the eyes of unconditional love and without judgment. At birth, we saw everything through the eyes of wonder and curiosity. While the old saying, "curiosity killed the cat," may be bad news for cats, it does not old true for us. We came into this world fully open to receive all that came before us, and we perceived everything with wonder and awe. There was no judgment about anything. The things in our lives either worked for our well-being or they did not; we spent no time in judgment of those things.

As time went on, we learned how to judge. We adopted judgements and beliefs from our parents, schools, religions, governments, television and many other areas. We truly are like sponges and absorb many things that are occurring around us, especially as children. We created the habit of judging at an early age and carry it with us into every situation in life. Our judgments act as filters through which we see the world and the life occurring around us. While many judgments may seem to be beneficial to us, they are not, they merely hinder our ability to see the truth of the situations or people we are judging.

The observations we made as children and the beliefs we created around them became judgments and shape the world we see. These judgments, whether we created them or adopted them from others, are now embedded in our subconscious and affect our lives each day.

The good news is that we learned this behavior. We learned how to emulate the judgments of others, and we learned how to create our own. We have been excellent learners, too. The better news is that we have proven we can learn and because of this truth, we can learn a new way of perceiving all of life. We can learn how to move beyond the judgments that serve only to limit our experience of life and find new ways of responding.

When we resurrect the ability to mindfully perceive, without judgment, all that is happening in our lives and our relationships, we again see what works and what does not. We can see the good and intentions of the situations and people instead of the limiting judgment. It is in judgment of the situations and actions of others that we stifle our own ability to learn and grow, to elevate and expand. In judgment we cheat ourselves from the fullness of life.

This journey you are beginning with The Relationship Toolbox is a judgment free experience. Releasing judgments opens you to the full experience and discovery of what your relationship, and your life, can truly be.

It is important to understand that the time you spend with this book is merely the first step in the journey to elevate and expand your relationship, and when the actual journey of elevating and expanding love in your relationship is free of judgment, you will grow personally and elevate your relationship. One of the most common judgments in a journey like this is that once you complete the book, you are done, and all will be well. If this thought, this judgment pops up for you, let it go, take it to the curb.

You will be served well by continuing the practice as you explore these tools each and every day. In fact, the real benefit of these tools comes after you complete the book and put the tools and considerations into practice in your life and relationship.

The tool, "Leave Your Judgments at the Curb," is possibly the most powerful practice you can begin. The title for this tool is appropriate as the curb is where trash is left to be hauled away. Judgments in our relationships are little more than trash that many of us hoard until there is no room for anything new. When we fill our minds with judgments, we greatly hinder our ability to see truth, to experience newness and to experience peace. When we judge, we are using our past experiences, the baggage, and things we learned, as a litmus test for what is happening around us. This is where we determine something as good or bad; right or wrong.

We often form judgment long before the situation has completely unfolded and cheat ourselves and our partners from the full experience that is available. Judgments serve only to cloud our vision and block the goodness of the situation. Even in those instances where goodness may very well seem to be small or non-existent, judgments prevent us from seeing the opportunities to heal and grow. The judgments we carry blind us from the opportunities that are available.

When we release judgments, we can easily see something as working or not working, and from that perception, we can move forward and shift everything that is going on in our lives, especially in our relationships.

The largest issue with judging is that it is usually used toward something negative and in judging the negative, we create an atmosphere of negativity. We add to the negativity in the situation. What is important to know is that there is good in everything. Judgment holds us prisoner to the illusion that things are bad, wrong or broken. When we view a situation or action without judgement, we can see the good that is there even if the situation or action does not serve us or our relationships. When we view without judgement, even if we are unable to see good in the action or situation, we can see good in our partners and ourselves.

In judging, possibility is hindered. In judging, growth is limited. In judging, healing and the well-being of our relationship, our partner and ourselves are stifled if not completely destroyed. Even if we never outwardly express our judgment, we greatly harm our ability to experience all that is available for us and our relationships.

When judgement is expressed outwardly, blame comes to visit. When blame is allowed, it is usually aimed at our partners for all that we judge as wrong in the relationship. Judgment says our partners are not who we hoped they would be. Judgement attacks their actions or inactions. Judgement goes after their behaviors and their habits. Judgement eventually warps our perception of our partners true selves and we see their personality traits as wrong.

When we judge, we tend to judge every aspect of our partner's life. We judge them as a person and we judge their participation in relationship itself. When we judge and blame, we put ourselves in victim mentality. When we find ourselves a victim, we are seeing ourselves with no power. In victim mode, we have no ability to change things for good, we convince ourselves we have no ability to elevate love in the relationship and this usually rolls over into other aspects of our lives as well. When we fall into victim mentality, we certainly can't expect growth and enrichment in our relationship.

Consider this for a moment. There are no victims, only volunteers. The simple truth of this statement is that even though we do not always have control over what happens in our lives, or in this case, our relationships, we always, without exceptions, have control over how we perceive and respond to that which happens to us. How we respond makes us heroes or victims in our own lives. When we find ourselves in unwanted or painful situations we can choose, or volunteer, to be a victim or we can choose to be a hero of our circumstances. It really is a choice.

Choosing to be a hero and releasing judgment is a conscious decision and one we can make in each moment of the day. We empower ourselves to create a judgment free life when we open our awareness to the thoughts and feelings we have in every situation. Mindfully tuning in to what is going on within allows us to let go of the limiting and damaging judgments that hold us in the pain.

Just as judgments were learned from the people and world around us, opening to the amazing possibilities found in judgment-free living can be learned as well. We can create new pathways of thought by simply opening awareness to our thoughts. Our thoughts create an emotional charge within us. This emotional charge becomes our beliefs. Our beliefs empower our actions, and our actions lead to our results. Ultimately, our thoughts become our reality.

We no longer need to carry around the burden of holding judgment, we can learn a healthier way of responding to life. We can be free, and it is a choice. When we make this choice, all of life and our relationships begin to heal around us.

Compare No More

A subset of judgment is comparison. For the most part, we are a people driven by external motivation. We look to the world to determine what is right and good, and our relationships are no different. Very few of us do not compare our relationship or ourselves, to others. There are many ways to compare, especially in relationships, and you may not even realize you are doing it.

By simply being human, we are tempted to compare and even feel that we are obligated to compare in many cases. The temptation is to hold ourselves and our relationship, our home, our cars, basically everything in our life, up for comparison. We are tempted from deep within to see how we measure up to others. We even feel that comparison is necessary so that we can see how we rate against others, and it is easy to claim that comparison is a tool used to improve our lives.

Comparing is the driving force behind many industries these days. The fitness industry is primarily built on people comparing their physique to the physique of others. The automobile industry was originally built on providing transportation from point A to point B but is now an industry comparing their product to another product and diligently working to convince you that they win in the comparison. Society demands we compare ourselves, our relationship and our entire lives to others, and if we come out anywhere other than on top we must go back to the drawing board and try again and buy again.

It has been said that the comparison of products creates a healthy market place. This does not hold true in our relationships. Comparing ourselves and our relationships leads only to an unwinnable pursuit. When we compare ourselves or our relationship to others, we set ourselves up to fail every time.

When we look within ourselves, to our essence, and face the truth, we realize that comparing is not the empowering act we first believed it to be. Comparing anything about us is usually a sign of insecurity and weakness. In the very best comparison scenarios, comparing serves only to rate us or our relationship better or worse than another. When we see a difference in value between ourselves and another, whether that be ourselves or our relationship or anything else for that matter, what we are seeing is the illusion of separation, the façade of lack. In separation and lack we see perceived short-comings.

When we find ourselves worse off than another we see our relationship, ourselves or our stuff as less than or inferior. When we see others as the lesser by comparison, we tend to move into one of two behaviors. When we see our relationships as better we either become relaxed and rest in the comfort found there or we move into the need to continue working diligently to out-pace the relationship to which we compared.

In relaxing into the comfort of "being better" we cheat ourselves, our partner and our relationship of newness. We stop seeking ways to find ways to elevate and expand the relationship. In seeking to out-pace the other relationships, we become so focused on moving ahead that we tend to leave out the expansion of love for our partner.

Comparison is always found when we look outside of ourselves for the definition of how we are meant to be.

Comparison blinds us to what we already have and the beauty that is found in the connection between our partners and ourselves. When we compare, we get tunnel vision for the external answers and fail to see the good we already have. When we forget that our truth is found within, we search far and wide only to move further from our truth and deeper into comparison to others. Comparison will never serve our highest good, personally or relationally.

Unfortunately, the act of comparing, when it comes to our partners, our relationships and even ourselves, has become one of the most common behaviors in our lives. It has become a tool of sorts, although a misguided one, that we use to better our relationships or end them. It has become an addiction in many cases in the constant search for something more.

While I am a fan of elevating and expanding relationships, and all of life for that matter, comparison is not the way to get it done.

Comparing our partner to someone else is not always about seeing our partner's shortcomings; it can also be about seeing how much better off we have it with them than with someone else. It really can begin innocently enough and as long as gratitude is involved, it may even feel healthy to a point. The line though between healthy and damaging is very hard to notice until we have passed over it and that is often too late.

For instance, a healthy comparison may be when you see a man lustfully staring at someone other than his spouse, you can be grateful for the fact that your husband does not do that. If you see a woman ripping into her husband for glancing at his smart phone one too many times at dinner, you can be thankful that your wife does not express her feelings in such a way.

Seeing things like this from a place of gratitude is not a simple case of comparing; gratitude is the primary behavior. However, when gratitude takes a back seat in this observation, we find comparison. It is when we raise or lower the value we hold for our partner as compared to others that this all becomes a problem. When actions of others cause us to like our spouse more or lead us to become more irritated with them, this all becomes comparison and ultimately a problem for the relationship. In the comparison, we stop seeing our partner for who they are and begin rating them as we would a product.

The truth is that comparing, when done often enough, will turn into a habit. When the habit of comparing is present while having a rough day or two in the relationship, we can easily fall into the negative comparisons where we see traits we wish our partner had more of, and we can see traits we wish our partner did not have at all. When this happens, we begin to see lack in our partner which translates into lack in the relationship and from there, who knows where it will all end up before we get a handle on our perceptions again.

To be clear; being grateful for our partners' healthier behaviors elevates the love in our relationships. When we open our awareness to these behaviors and traits without comparison, we steer clear of that near invisible line between gratitude and comparison. Comparison is rarely a positive action even when the initial intent is one of gratitude, so instead of going there, we can choose to hold our partner in gratitude only. We can choose to see all the ways they contribute to the love and happiness within the relationship.

If we do see lack in the relationship or our partner, we can ask for what we need without comparing them to others. Most importantly, we can be sure that above all things love and gratitude for our partner and the relationship are present.

Having said all that, I know that it is easy to compare, and many times comparison can sneak into our daily behaviors. Our culture has taught us to compare everything in our lives. The advertising world teaches us that we must compare everything because when we compare, they get to sell. They have us compare our car to the car on their commercial. Televisions shows have us compare the lives of the made-up family to our own in order to create comedy or drama; it all depends on what they are selling. Religion asks you to compare to other religions and then point out why theirs is better. It all goes on and on and in all honesty, it simply wears us out.

So, before we move away from the topic of comparison, let's look at how comparison may show up as an active practice in a relationship.

> We sometimes compare our partner to someone else.
> We compare our partner to our father or mother.
> We compare our relationship to the relationships on television shows and in movies.
> We compare our partner to society's definition of the perfect partner.
> We hold them up in comparison to the potential we think we see in them.
> We compare them to our own definition of the perfect partner.

➢　　We compare our relationship and our partner to what religion defines as the perfect example.

I have had conversations where people compare their spouse to a friend's spouse... "Well if my wife looked like Charlie's..." or "Samantha's husband is so much more loving than my husband."

First of all we are totally de-valuing our partner every time we do this. *(We are also totally de-valuing our relationship and ourselves when we do this.)* Even if we never do this in front of them, they will feel it through the way we look at them and treat them.

How can we truly compare anyway? In the example above, the truth may be that Charlie's wife is a total terror behind closed doors and Samantha's husband may be cheating on her when nobody is looking. We do not know the whole truth and we probably never will so even if comparing was a good idea, which it is not, we cannot get apples to apples comparison, ever.

Also, there are no two people just alike anywhere on this planet. Out of more than seven billion people breathing air on this planet, no other person is like your partner. Even if your partner is an identical twin, each of the twins have had different experiences and perceptions in their own individual lives so they truly cannot be compared to each other or anyone else.

Have you ever caught yourself comparing your partner to someone else's definition of the ideal partner? Have you ever heard your friends or co-workers describe their idea of the perfect partner and thought, hmmmm? When we buy into what someone else is saying, it is easy to see their definition as true. We then come to believe that the only way our relationship can work is for our partner to change and become that person described by our friend. It then becomes extremely easy to overlook the awesome and unique qualities our partner brings to the relationship; you know, those things we fell in love with in the first place. When we forget those things, it is easy to get upset when our partner falls short of all we thought they should be.

Sometimes we compare our current partner to past partners. This one always tickles me. Imagine for a moment when you first met your current partner. You may have been thrilled by many of the traits and characteristics this partner had that your past partners did not have. You may find that something you hated about your former partner is not present in your current partner.

At some point, we begin comparing the partners. Even if the comparison is to see that the current partner does not do the irritating things that our past partners did, we are putting our partners in the same boat and nothing good can come of that.

This becomes a mental jousting match. We put our partners, past and present on the same field and let them fight it out to see who will win the right to be with us. Chances are that since we are focusing on all of the negative of our past partners we will automatically be drawn to the negatives of our current partner. How much stress will that put on the relationship?

What does it tell our current partner when we compare them to a past partner? Even if we are only considering the negative traits of our past partner, the fact that we are thinking of them could very well tell our current partner we prefer to be with our old lover. We could very well be sending a subliminal message that this relationship is doomed.

So just do not go there. Leave comparison out of the mix. This current partner brings something to the relationship or there never would have been a relationship in the first place. They are unique and have their own individuality to offer you and the relationship. Again, see the individual and do not devalue your current partner by holding them up in comparison to a past relationship.

Another way we fall into comparison is to compare our partner to a character we have seen on a favorite TV show. I imagine that if your current partner had a team of writers to script every action and every word, a director to make sure they get it right, and a producer to fund it all, they too would not falter too much in the relationship department. But maybe that too would fail as the only way a writer could get it perfectly right would be if they scripted your life as well, so they could control your reactions to the things they wrote for your partner to do. Please remember, your life and your relationship are not TV and TV relationships are not real in most cases. In those TV relationships that are based on true stories, comparison is still a set-up for failure as they are not you or your partner and they are written from a biased point of view. (*The point of view of whoever paid to have the show made*)

Another way we compare our partner is to see how they stack up against someone who has had a long and healthy relationship. Your friends, parents or grandparents may be examples you use. If you want to go and talk to people who have had great success over a long period of time in the relationship area of life, then do so. It is great to hear some of the things that made their relationship a success. Just remember to tweak their words of wisdom to fit your own relationship.

Notice though, that I did not say go and talk to them just to compare relationships. Nor did I say to go as a way of learning how to change your partner to be like that person's partner. Those things will never work because all you will accomplish in doing that is to tell your partner that you believe them to be so broken that you had to seek out wisdom on how to fix them.

One of my favorite relationship jokes, which is not really that funny because it holds much truth, goes something like this:

> *Soon after we got married I was told to change the way I dressed. My current style was outdated, shabby; not at all what our friends were wearing and miles away from current styles.*
>
> *I changed.*
>
> *I was then told to change jobs for better pay and status. Even though the new job would require many extra hours, the pay was much better and would allow us to live the lifestyle we saw on our favorite show and we could now "keep up with the Joneses."*
>
> *I changed.*
>
> *I was then told to change my hair style. The one I had was not mature and stylish enough.*
>
> *I changed.*
>
> *I was told to listen to different music. I apparently needed to grow up and listen to age appropriate music. Our friends did not listen to the kind I liked.*
>
> *I changed.*

*I was then told that I had changed so much
that I just was not myself anymore. My partner just
could not live with me any longer and left.*

This happens very frequently.

Another way we hold our partner up in comparison is
when we pick up the habit of comparing them to the person
they were when we first met them. How de-valuing is that?
Of course, they will not be the same. Growth expands and
elevates the person and the relationship. When we see the
growth, they experience with love and gratitude it can fuel
and encourage positive growth in the relationship and within
us as well. Our partner will grow and change no matter what
we do. They will grow just as we will grow so embrace that
change; encourage that change. Allow and accept the
changes to empower the relationship.

Your partner is simply a person that has his or her
own personality just as you do. Cherish the person you fell
for initially and at the same time, allow that person to grow
each day. Who they were in the beginning is part of your
relationship's foundation. Who they grow into strengthens
the foundation. Appreciate the growth, support the growth
and see the beauty it can bring to the relationship. Enjoy
their journey and encourage their journey. After all, you are
also on a journey and this part of your journey is intertwined
with this part of theirs.

To recap, comparing is done for many reasons and
not too many of them are pretty. We tend to compare to
make our own situations appear better. We sometimes
compare as a way of deflecting attention away from
something we see as lacking. We sometimes compare to
show our partner where they are falling short in their part of
the relationship. When things are not going well, we

compare our relationship to others in order to prove that we are not where we think the relationship should be. This often moves into a blame game where our partner is at fault for the lack we think we see in the relationship.

Comparing only serves to de-value the person and the relationship. Comparing is unfair and involves people and situations from totally different backgrounds and life experiences. Comparing eats away at the foundation of what brought you and your partner together and will crumble the entire relationship. Comparing can sneak in and cause you to forget what it was that you fell in love with in the first place. So, if you are in a relationship and this has begun, look for the positive traits in your spouse and leave comparison out of the mix. Hold on to the love and drop the comparing.

Comparing serves no purpose in any relationship. Actually, it serves no purpose in most of life and we have only tricked ourselves into thinking we need to compare so we can rate ourselves, our partners and our relationships.

We compare ourselves to others as well. We tend to rank our own personal value as individuals based on what we see in others. We are either okay or not okay depending on how we stack up against our friends or characters we see on television and what main stream media tells us is okay or not okay.

While this book is devoted to relationships, I want to pause for a moment and challenge you to tune into how often you compare yourself to others. Become aware of how you do it, what triggers you to do it and what kind of things you tell yourself when you fall into this behavior. Once you become aware of it remember this, "You are unique and cannot be compared to anyone or anything else. You lack nothing and need only to allow the perfection of you, which means all of you, to shine."

This is the truth: you are unique and there will never be any way you can do an apples to apples comparison to anyone else, so do not devalue yourself by comparing. As long as you are devaluing yourself by comparing, you have little hope of working on this very important tool in your relationship. Compare no more is a tool for you individually as much, and maybe even more, than it is for your relationship. See yourself for the amazing person you are, and you can begin to create, maintain or renew the amazing relationship you deserve.

Comparison is over rated. Comparing products and services can be beneficial; comparing individuals only tears people down and creates the illusion of lifting others up. Most importantly, when we compare people we are forced into judgment and in judgment we limit our ability to know the whole truth about a person or ourselves.

Compare no more and embrace the truth of you, your partner and your relationship. Releasing comparison invites you to realize the amazing uniqueness you have in your life.

Release Expectations

Once we become aware of the ways in which we judge or compare our partner, our relationship and ourselves, we empower ourselves to stop the behaviors. When we mindfully choose to stop judging or comparing, we have made great strides in opening space for our relationships to elevate and expand. Even though we have made the choice to leave our judgments by the curb and compare no more, we still have a little more releasing to do.

Throughout our lives we have learned and created expectations. These expectations are an extension of our judgments and comparisons. They come to us from the impressions our former judgments and comparisons have made within our subconscious.

Expectations can serve as a benefit when we practice manifestation and positive affirmations; however, they serve us best when we acknowledge them and then release them. This allows for all we expect and more to come to us. While we are holding tightly to the expectation, we limit what may come that we have not imagined yet. While we focus on expectations, we may miss the manifestation of them if they do not manifest for us exactly as we vision them.

We create expectations in many ways. We have expectations that are based on past results. We have expectations that are based on our experience in different situations that seem like the one we are currently experiencing. In short, the expectations we are describing here, are beliefs that something will occur in response to something else.

Let's first address the expectations we have when manifesting or positive affirmations. One of the keys to manifesting that which we desire is belief that it is coming to us. We must have some expectation of what that will be, or we will never attract that thing into our lives. When we are practicing positive affirmations, we must expect that statement to be our truth. These expectations serve and assist us in manifesting the situation or thing we desire.

Even in the situations where we may be using expectations to assist in strengthening our belief around a goal or intention, we are greatly served by allow something more to develop. We can only receive something more if we release the expectation that assisted us in creating the affirmation or vision. When we hold tight to the expectation and discount anything that does not seem identical to our vision, we cheat ourselves of something better.

The expectations we are addressing here, though, are limiting at best and often damage our relationships, our partners and ourselves.

One of the ways in which this happens is in our relationship is when something happens, and we hold a specific expectation of the outcome. It may be when we say a something and expect a certain response from our partner. We all have expectations of our partner and their behaviors. We have expectations of our relationships and yes, we even have expectations of ourselves.

Expectations prevent us from being completely mindful and present in our relationship. They place us in the past and force us to compare. When we expect our partner, relationship, or self to react or respond in certain ways, we cheat ourselves from what is occurring in the present moment, and we cheat ourselves of something wonderfully new and different that may be coming our way. When we look for the expected reaction, we often are blind to the new and refreshing response that comes our way.

Now, expectations are not completely wrong or damaging. This brings us back to the expectations around manifesting goodness and positivity. When we set expectations from a place of love and we look for things that will serve highest good, we can easily classify them as intentions. With intentions, we allow for that new something to occur. When we set our intentions and include flexibility; we allow presence and mindfulness to open awareness to the truth of the response. We must be open to experience what comes our way.

In expectations we find comfort. In allowing without expectations, we feel vulnerable. In truth, vulnerability is stepping far outside of our comfort zones. However, in this vulnerability we are in a position to allow all that may come. We allow goodness that our expectation may not include. We allow love that may be absent in the expectations we hold.

When we leave our comfort zone, we leave normal status behind. When we leave our comfort zones, we expand and elevate our life experience. Each time we leave our comfort zone, very quickly our comfort zone expands, and the fear associated with vulnerability eases. And then, we are empowered to do it all over again.

This chapter could easily have been named "Replace Expectations with Intentions." Beginning with expectations can be an empowering process when those expectations are focused on elevating love and our experience of life. Converting expectations to intentions opens us to more than we expect. We can expand the vision we have for our relationship and experience positive results when we allow for more than our expectations hold.

When you find yourself expecting the worst, when you think something bad will come to you in a situation, release that belief. Just let it go and replace it with expectations or intentions of something wonderful. What you believe, whether good or bad, will be your experience. Expectations often hold us in the negative while intentions elevate us into the positive.

Leave Your Judgments at the Curb, Compare No More and Release Expectations. When you do this, you elevate and expand yourself, your relationship, and you give permission to your partner to live more fully in their essence. Even if your partner is not traveling this journey with you, they, too, will experience the shift that takes place in your release and you will see them grow as well.

Stop Making Stuff Up

When we get very honest with ourselves, we will find that we tend to make stuff up frequently. We make stuff up about people and the things they say. We make stuff up about things, feelings, experiences and just about anything else that occurs in life. We even make stuff up about ourselves all the time. One of the ways we do this, but certainly not the only way, is when we give value to a limiting belief about ourselves.

We make something up about ourselves every time we allow one of those limiting or negative thoughts to take time and space in our mind. The thought rolls around in our mind until we create a story around it. From that thought we create a belief and many times that belief is based on nothing more than the story we made up. We do this way more often than we want to admit. Obviously, we like to think that our interpretation of the thoughts in our head, the messages sent by others and the situations in our lives are correct. Many times, though, those interpretations are nothing but conjecture.

Have you ever walked through a shopping center and made up stuff about people you see? We often see someone else shopping and make up stuff about their ability to purchase an item they may be looking over. We make up stuff about what they do for a living based on the clothes they wear. We make up stuff about their political beliefs, their hobbies, their likes and dislikes all from a glance.

How about seeing that long haired guy covered in tattoos that just pulled up next to you on his extremely loud motorcycle? What is made up about him? What did the number of piercings on the girl standing in front of you in the check-out line invite your mind to make up about her? In my experience, as much fun as making stuff up can be, discovering the truth usually is way more interesting.

When we catch ourselves making stuff up about someone or even about situations, we must prevent the illusions we made up from becoming our belief about them. As much fun as it may be sometimes, it is still making stuff up and until there is factual proof of the truth of that person, we are believing a fabrication.

Making stuff up is present even in our relationships. Even though it is easy to believe that we know all there is to know about our partners and our relationships, we still make stuff up. When our partner tells us something, it is very easy to make stuff up about what they mean instead of gaining clarification. It is easy for an action to mean one thing, yet we make up something totally off-base and allow that to become our perception.

Often our makeup behaviors begin with a feeling that something is not what it seems. Think of a time your partner came home from work in a different mood than normal. What did you make up about them and what they may have been dealing with before asking for clarification? Did you actually ask for clarification? What stories did you make up if they answered, "Nothing," but did not change their disposition?

In our relationships we do not necessarily make up stuff about the surface level stuff like where our partners work or where they are from; we do it on a much deeper level and actually try our hand at reading their minds and emotions. Unfortunately, most of us are not tapped into our psychic powers, so no matter how we try to justify our actions, this really ends up being nothing more than making stuff up.

Here are some questions that may assist you in knowing when you are making stuff up in your relationship:

> Where does your mind go when your partner looks at you a little differently than usual?
> What do you think when they are unusually quiet or distant?
> What thoughts jump into your mind when their tone of voice is a little more harsh than normal?
> Do you run different scenarios through your mind of what might have happened to cause this odd behavior or what is wrong with them?
> Do you have several different scenarios running through your head about what is about to happen?
> Do you automatically assume it is something you did that caused this?
> Do you begin coming up with exit strategies to avoid the impending doom of what is to come?
> What does your mind do when your partner is late from work; before they arrive home or report in?

The key to stop making stuff up is to open awareness to the thoughts running through your head. Sound familiar? We open our awareness to judgments, comparison, and expectations in order to release them, we do the same with making stuff up.

Notice the change in all of these tools is a change that is happening within ourselves, within you. This is not a book about how to change your partner, it is about opening to the authentic you by opening awareness and then adjusting your behaviors and reactions. With these changes and adjustments, you will experience a shift towards the relationship and life you desire.

When you pay attention to your thoughts, it is easy to recognize when you are making stuff up. Once you become aware of a thought in your mind, you can ask, "Is it true and can this truth I believe be supported with evidence?" One of the greatest resources available to you comes in the form of a question; "What am I thinking now?" Tune in to how you feel in the moment. Is the feeling appropriate?

If what you are making up brings, fear, anger, hurt or any other negative feeling you stand the chance of allowing that feeling, whether justified or not, to interfere with the relationship between you and your partner. Those negative feelings can even become so consuming that the gravitational pull of that emotion grabs hold of anyone else that may be in the household, and even friends and family, as well.

Many unnecessary fights and elevated levels of tension are common when one or both partners are making stuff up. The conflicts and tensions may even escalate into full out battles when we begin predicting what our partner is thinking or about to do.

So, "Stop Making Stuff Up!" It serves no purpose. Whether the stuff you are making up goes to positive scenarios or gloom and doom scenarios, it is still making stuff up and does not serve you, the relationship or your partner.

The question often arises as to how making up positive scenarios can be a negative thing. First, it cheats us out of experiencing the present moment; we miss what is really happening. And, what is really happening may be far

52

better than what we are making up. Also, the positive illusion can quickly turn into a negative when we start believing what we made up; we are creating a new truth based on the imaginings of our minds. When the true intentions of the person or the true impact of the situation comes to light and is different than what we have come to believe, we feel lied to and betrayed. Of course, this is all happening within our own mind and sometimes our own heart, however, it feels real and real emotions and feelings come to the surface. There really is no "okay" way to make stuff up unless you can stay completely aware that it is all made up.

As easy as it is to manufacture these illusions, the question becomes, how do we perceive and stay in truth? We must open mindful awareness of the present moment. We must first find out what is really going on with the person or situation. We do that through communications which we will discuss later in this book. We mindfully open awareness by becoming curious without judgment, comparison or expectations.

So, if your partner looks at you differently, is a little harsher and so on, it may simply mean that they had a bad day and have not sorted it all out yet. They may simply feel out of sorts. They may just be tired or even a bit under the weather. The point is we will never know the truth until we stop making stuff up, tune in to them to find out or ask what is going on. If their answer is "nothing," it may very well be nothing. If they are the type to say "nothing" just to avoid talking about it, let them know you care and you are there to chat about it if and when they are ready. You may want to use a phrase similar to, "I sense that you are upset about something, and I just wanted to check in to see if there is anything I can do." Approach the person and the topic with love and caring and then step back after making the statement and allow them to feel support.

Be careful of your phrasing though. A phrase similar to this, "I feel like you are upset, and it makes me feel... fill in the blank," may easily drive a wall between you and them. This phrasing tends to lay blame on them. It makes them responsible for your feelings. It is a little selfish and could put them on the defensive which does not work well to get answers or assist them in feeling better.

Sometimes it is okay to simply allow them to have their feelings as long as the relationship is not being harmed. Be patient and allow space for them to process whatever is going on. If it gets to the point that damage occurs, you owe it to you, the relationship and your partner to begin a conversation. Just be sure to leave out the blaming, finger pointing, anger, fear or any other negativity that could derail the conversation. Keep it loving, authentic and open to discussion. Give them the opportunity to talk it out with you. Listen to what they have to say and tune in to the feelings they are experiencing.

Of course, if you just told yourself that you can never find the courage to have that conversation, you are making stuff up about you. You are perfectly capable of finding a way to talk to your partner. When you center you into love and peace and express from that place, you can have the conversation. In fact, centering yourself in love and peace will strengthen and guide you in every situation when you allow it. Stop Making Stuff Up!

Re-Commit with Realistic Commitments

If you feel that you are ready to release what no longer serves, leave your judgments by the curb, compare no more, release expectations and stop making stuff up, you are truly ready to elevate your relationship. While there are a more tools that will serve you and your relationship still to come, now is a good time for an internal check-in... Are you ready to re-commit to your relationship?

I can hear it now, Ugh! I committed once when I got into this relationship. I can hear it especially loud form some of you married folks out there who made a public statement of your commitment at your wedding. Some of you may have even renewed your vows since the original declaration of love and commitment. As with the tools presented in this book, commitment to your relationship is an on-going process.

With the dawn of each new day, we begin a new journey of life and relationship. Commitment is something that is required each day; each moment of the day. Commitment is not a once and done thing. Life circumstances, our relationships and ourselves, are constantly changing and require renewed commitment all along the way. The difference between the time when original commitments were made and now is that you are learning valuable tools to assist you in elevating the authenticity of your part in the relationship, as well as life.

You will now see the relationship and your partner differently than ever before. You will see yourself differently than ever before. You are invited to re-commit to experiencing and expressing from a place of authenticity and love that may not have been noticable before.

I frequently hear how committed someone is to the relationship. It is easy to speak this statement, not so easy to live this statement. Once we make the commitment to be in the relationship and to love our partner, we often allow the intensity of our commitment to fade a bit. We adopt the once and done mentality. We begin to take the status of our relationship for granted and we begin to see our partner less and less as the person we fell in love with and more as a roommate with benefits. And, if we stay in this frame of mind long enough the benefits even begin to disappear.

An ever-growing relationship is about re-committing every day. I am not saying to commit to being just like you were yesterday. Even if everything seemed perfect yesterday, committing each day means to commit to being and giving more of your heart and love more than the day before. It is bringing the wiser, more experienced self into the relationship. It is about growing and offering the benefits of that growth to our partner and the relationship.

Each day, we commit to love a little deeper. We commit to smile a little broader. We commit to express ourselves a little more authentically. We commit to laugh a little more lovingly. We commit to listen deeper than mere words. We commit to be better than we were the day before and find a way to make the relationship stronger than it ever has been.

Impossible you say? Not at all. When traveling a journey of a thousand miles, when we hit that last mile, we can see thousands of more miles to travel; if we choose.

There are opportunities for deeper love and expanded growth in each moment of the day. Our journey never ends, it merely transitions as we go. Our entire universe is made of deeper and deeper levels; we have the physical levels, the energetic, the emotional and the spiritual. Each one of these levels is ever expanding, ever deepening and forever elevating.

To test this theory, take a walk into nature. Look around and take in all you see. When you think you have seen it all, take another step and look again. From this perspective you can see more. Some things are being seen for the first time and others are being seen from a new perspective. When you think you have seen it all from here, take a new step and repeat.

Once you have done this several times move closer to the area you are observing. As you close the gap leaves on the trees will look different, blades of grass will be seen as individual reeds instead of a carpet of green, the bark of the tree begins to show its texture and stones reveal their beauty in brand new ways.

When we authentically look closer at ourselves, our partners and our relationships we will see that everything has many more levels than we initially realized. Some of what we see are changes that have occurred since we first met our partners, some are different perceptions of what we saw at first. Some of the new levels we see in our partners and relationships are much deeper than we thought to look, and all are evolving each day. When we can open our hearts, minds, eyes and our entire being to this truth, it becomes easy to commit, or re-commit, to expanding our participation in the relationship.

While it is essential to continue positive-growth through commitment, there are other types of commitments that need to be addressed and avoided. Here are some commitment pitfalls to keep in your awareness:

Committing just to make them happy- Sometimes our desire to make our partner happy leads the way when it comes to commitment. This pitfall seems to come from a place of love but be very careful here. Often, it is really coming from a place of fear. Fear that we will lose our partner if we do not make the commitment. We fall into an insecurity that they will no longer love us as much if we do not take care of this issue and so on. As this illusion continues, we make more promises and take more onto our plate; and our plate is often already overflowing.

It is important to know that nothing we do can actually make our partner happy or unhappy. They get to choose the feeling they will experience on their own. They are responsible for their own feelings. Now, having said all that, if we want to do something for them out of the kindness of our heart, perfect; we can do it out of love for them and not out of a feeling of being responsible for their happiness.

Committing without knowing what we are committing to - Okay, this is one we rarely admit too but most of us do it. We are in the middle of something and our partner begins chatting away about something they would like to do, and we just nod our heads and agree and before we know it we have committed to something and really have no idea that we have done it. While the general belief is that men are the ones guilty of this practice, do not be fooled. Ladies, you do it too.

Many times, it starts out innocently enough and even with good intention. Even though we are interested in whatever we are doing at the time, our partner is important enough to us that we want to listen to what they have to say.

58

Instead of asking for them to hold off until we are done or put our task on hold, we simply do our best to listen while still doing what we were doing in the first place.

No matter how great a job we think we did in the listening department, we did not hear all that was said, and we certainly did not hear any of the "between the lines" meaning. By not fully tuning into our partner, we not only commit to things without the full picture, chances are we also cheated ourselves out of fully experiencing the thing we were doing when we tried to multi-task.

When we experience this communication breakdown, we often find ourselves in trouble for forgetting about what we committed to do and then struggle to discover what we are missing. We may have missed a key factor of the process due to the half listening. Sometimes we hear the overall project and totally miss the reasons and feelings that are just as, if not more, important than the actions asked of us.

Now, there is another version of this scenario and that is committing to our partners just to shut them up, so we can get back to what we were doing in the first place. If this is a practice in your relationship, STOP. STOP IT NOW! This is inconsiderate, rude, mean, and cruel, and I could go on and on. We must be willing to communicate fully by stopping what we are doing so we can tune in to our partner or asking to have the conversation at a later time.

Committing because we "should." A dear friend of mine has a saying she shares with her friends and clients, "Stop 'Shoulding' All Over the Place." Embedded within our egos is a little voice that tells us we "should" do this and we "should" do that. Our entire life has been filled with people telling us or demonstrating to us how we should act, and react, to different scenarios in life. We are excellent learners and picked these lessons up and have integrated them into our sub-conscious, and they are active all the time.

When we commit to something because we "should," we fail to consider what may serve highest good in the situation. Sometimes, the thing asked of us will serve highest good, however, sometimes, it does not. When we open our awareness to all things that deserve consideration - our partner, the relationship, ourselves, etc. - we will see how best to commit or if we need to at all.

Committing with no intention to follow through- This scenario is another of those that is used to shut someone up. We may not be able to fulfill the commitment, we may not have time to hear the request, and we may not have any desire to do what is being asked, so we just agree so the conversation will be over.

While the immediate peace of making a commitment can be very nice, the chaos that comes from not fulfilling the commitment overrides that peace in a hurry. This is one of the cruelest examples of how to treat a partner, or anyone else as far as that goes.

A simple no instead of a misleading commitment would have been the better answer. Yes, it may have caused anger, sadness or other negative responses. Yes, it may have brought on a whole different conversation to deal with. Yes, there may have been other negative issues that popped up; however, there is still no legitimate reason to treat someone or ourselves with this lack of respect.

When we find ourselves in a position where we have no time to hear the request, instead of committing with no intention of following through, we can simply ask to have the chat later and schedule it. If the request is something we have no desire or ability to fulfill, instead committing with no intention of following through, we can explain to our partner the truth that we cannot or will not do it.

We obviously care for the person asking for the commitment. Even if we cannot do it ourselves, we can possibly assist them in finding a way to get it done. We can give them some ideas of people who can help. We can share our ideas of where to look for results. The key in this one is to not compromise our integrity. Instead, we can stay true to the authenticity we bring to the relationship. We serve the relationship and our partner best when we stay true to our essence and let our hearts lead the way.

To re-commit and make realistic commitments, we must consider the request, our partner, our relationship and ourselves. We must be certain we are in a position to make the commitment. It is much easier to say no on the front end than back out or make a change later. Before committing, we honor ourselves and our partners by taking a moment; understanding what we are committing to and knowing that we can honor the commitment with fulfillment of what we promised.

Obviously, there will be times when we whole-heartedly make a commit and life decides to get in the way. When unforeseen situations arise that prevent us from following through, we must communicate immediately, or at least as soon as possible, with the person we committed to. It is our responsibility to let the person know the issue and see if there is any way we can change our commitment or postpone the end date until such time that we can complete the promise. Do not leave it hanging. Resentment, anger, major decline in trust levels and other not so pleasant things and emotions can arise when we do.

Know what you are committing to; know that you can complete it; know that you can lovingly participate in the project or action. Commitment can come from your heart, and when it does, it is beautiful.

Re-commit to you, your partner and your relationship and when you do, make realistic commitments. It is not your responsibility to take on the world or be more than you truly can be. Be you and allow commitments to be a gift you give and receive.

Be Your Authentic Self

Authentic: this is such a powerful and empowering word and a word that is often diluted by over-use. To know what being authentic really is, we must define it and consider how it applies in our life expression. The word authentic as defined by dictionaries means- "conforming to fact; therefore, worthy of trust, reliance or belief; having an undisputed origin."

Authentic, as referred to in this book, includes all of that and more; it is being the truth of ourselves. It is connecting wholeheartedly to our essence. It is experiencing and expressing all of life from that sacred space within. Wholeheartedly is found when we find balance between our hearts and minds. It is the connection of emotions and intellect and allowing both a voice in our considerations.

What authentic means for us as a person and as a part of a relationship is that as we live from our truth, our authentic self, we are trusting, loving, worthy and reliable.

Each and every one of us is conceived into this existence as a pure being; innocent and loving. At the point we became a human being, we were absolutely pure. There was nothing about us at that moment other than our authentic self. A saying that has been used in many places holds true here, "We are spiritual beings having an amazing human experience." In our spiritual truth, we are still pure, we are still loving and peaceful, we are authentic. As our human selves began to develop, we learned beliefs and behaviors that led us to the illusion that we are less than perfect; less than whole; less than worthy. As we aged, we allowed ourselves to be shaped by outside influences and often those influences fooled us into being something other than the truth that is our essence, our authentic self. That truth is still at our very core; it has just been masked by all that we told ourselves or heard from others about how we were supposed to be.

Even though it sounds quite difficult to tap back into and live as our authentic self, it is actually quite simple. Before getting to what being authentic is, let's talk a little about what it is not. It is not about trying to be something for someone else. It is not about putting up a facade and pretending to be something we are not. It is not about trying to be who everyone else thinks we should be. It is not about trying to be the person we saw on TV last night. It is not about being who our ego tells us we are. These serve no one and only hurts ourselves, our partner and the relationship.

Being authentic is about being true to our essence; our truth. This may not seem like much; however, it may be one of the greatest tools available for our experience and expression in relationships and all of life. Being authentic is about tapping into the essence that is at our core. This is the part of us where our internal guidance manifests; our intuition is birthed here. This is the part of us that we feel our deepest desires. This is the part of us that is connected to God, our source, the Universe, our higher power and our highest Self.

This is our truth. We are fully connected to a higher power and in that beautiful connection we are connected to all of creation. In this truth, we are perfect. When we all re-connect with this knowing, with this truth, we can let go of all the false personas and limiting beliefs we created about ourselves in order to be okay and fit in.

When we allow our authenticity a chance to take charge, we live from our heart. We follow where it leads. We open ourselves to happiness, peace and love. To be authentic is to come from that place deep within that is only love. Being authentic leaves judgment out of our lives, it kicks comparison out of the way and is open, caring, strong and courageous all at the same time.

Our relationships and our partners benefit greatly when we live as our authentic selves. When we share the strength, love, truth, joy, peace and the many other incredible attributes of our essence, our relationship has no choice but to expand and elevate.

Hiding from authenticity serves no purpose and only damages the relationship as well as ourselves. Constricting the amazing truth limits our growth and the growth of the relationship.

Be authentic; express love and peace into the relationship. Give love and peace to your partner. Give authentic love to you.

Work the Issues - Not Each Other

When we choose to be in a committed relationship, our daily dose of issues has a tendency to increase from what we experience while living a single lifestyle, and sometimes the increase is dramatic. The issues we all face as individuals become entangled with the issues being in a relationship entails and all that is further blended with the issues our spouse brings into the mix.

These Issues do not have to be difficult or negative; they can sometimes even be good things but the extra pressure on our schedules create a since of chaos. To better define issues in this instance, they are simply things we give our attention to throughout the day that take us away from our normal path. Sometimes we are distracted for a very brief moment, sometimes several minutes, other times hours. We can even become distracted by these issues for days or longer in certain circumstances. The nature of our relationship can increase the importance of some issues that were once trivial when we did not need to consider our partner or the relationship we share.

First of all, everyone, no matter what their relationship status, is first a person, an individual, and that in and of itself presents issues that we deal with every day. Life in general comes with many issues that we believe deserve our attention. Bills that need to be paid, traffic on our way to work, our government, health, entertainment and so much more; these are all part of the juggling act most of us deal with in our lives. Unless you have found enlightenment along your life journey, these issues can bring us to the brink of overwhelm once they begin to pile up.

More than a few people entered into a relationship with the belief that together, the issues would be easier to handle. And many of those people soon realized the opposite was true. A relationship carries with it its own set of issues. These issues only add to the issues you already face in life. Just as in the individual scenarios, the issues that occur in a relationship are not all negative. In fact, it is often easier to become overwhelmed when the positive things pile up. When facing numerous positive and fun activities in our schedule, we do not want to miss any, so we try even harder to make them happen; we fill our over full schedules with even more things.

In a relationship, when we think of food, we must now think for two. When we consider a movie to watch, we must consider our partner's likes and dislikes. While many people do not change their thought patterns when they enter a relationship, any hope of having a relationship that is healthy and expanding requires consideration of both people. Those who thought they could have an outstanding relationship but did not change their way of thinking just created a whole new set of issues that will need to be worked out.

Once again, these issues are not always bad things; they simply are things we must take into consideration. The new issues and considerations of a relationship do not replace the issues we once had as a single person, they do, though, cause our previous issues to shift a bit or change in importance.

Along with the individual issues and the additional issues related to being in a relationship we can add the issues our partners bring to the table. Our partner was once single and had their own set of issues just as we did. They bring those into the relationship just as we did. Put all this together and it is easy to understand why relationships seem so hard sometimes.

The issues do not define either of you nor do they define the relationship. They are simply things you must consider so that you and your partner can work through them and prevent them from becoming walls and sources of relationship break-down.

All too often, we allow the issues we face to define the person involved. We tend to allow a situation that angers us to bleed over into the person or persons involved in that situation. We allow the situation and the feelings associated with it to define the person. In relationships, this behavior easily escalates until it is difficult to see what we love about our partner through the wall of anger and frustration built by the issue.

"Work the Issues, Not Each Other" is a remember that we are not defined by the issues we face; and neither are our partners. Rather than seeing our partners as bad or wrong or broken in some way, we can give awareness to the issues we face. We can remember our partners are just that, our partners; they are not our enemy. Our partner can be our greatest ally when we focus on the issues instead of casting blame for the issue upon them.

"Work the Issues, Not Each Other" is a reminder to seek understanding of the issues before they become insurmountable mountains. Once we can see the issues for what they are, we can then decide how important they are in our lives and our relationship. We can determine how much of our energy or time they deserve. From this understanding, we can communicate with our partners to find agreement on what to do with it. The key to dealing with the issues we face is teaming with our partner to find understanding and then decide together how important it is. Together, we decide what needs to be done and then we, together, take appropriate action.

When we open awareness and attention, when we become mindful of what is going on in our relationship and with each other, we can identify the issues while they are small. We can work together as a couple and respond in healthy and loving ways. Ignoring the issues and allowing them to grow often creates overwhelm and it is here we find it easiest to lash out and blame. Unfortunately, our partners are usually the closest and easiest to attack.

Creating a safe way and a safe place to discuss the issues that appear in our relationships assists us in steering clear of the overwhelm. When we create this safe platform where we, as a team with our partners, can discuss the issues, we also create a resource that assists us in recognizing new issues that creep into the relationship. Early awareness, attention and intention to elevate the relationship removes the possibility for the issue to grow into a damaging problem. Get the issues out in the open and together discover what needs to be done.

"Work the Issues, Not Each Other" is about dealing with the issue itself. It is not about beating up on our partner; it is not about being right or winning. Working your partner is about a power struggle. Working the issue empowers both of you and the relationship.

Can we still work the issues and not each other when the situation becomes highly volatile? First of all, if you are unsafe or endangered in any way; seek safety. Once safe, you can begin to awaken to options and possibilities. An issue, no matter how calm or volatile it may be can never be resolved when we are in fear for our safety. We must find safety, so we can create a calm environment from which we can deal with the situation.

Physically abusive situations are not the only places we find volatile issues. Many couples stay together under the shadow of abuse on the emotional and mental realms. Many people believe that since there is no physical harm, there is no abuse. The effects of emotional and mental abuse are just as damaging if not more so than the physical abuse scenarios. These situations need attention as well.

The common way for people to deal with volatile issues is to use the "get them before they get me" behavior. This only escalates the tension and anger and does absolutely nothing to resolve the issue. To deal with these types of issues, again, seek a safe place. Once in a safe place, calm your heart and mind and know the issue is neutral and carries with it no power at all other than that you give it. This is not to say that another person is not threatening physical, mental or emotional attacks. It does mean, though, that it is not the issue that is wreaking havoc on our lives, it is our interpretation, our thoughts, our beliefs about the issue.

We have choices in how we perceive the situation and in how we respond. We can choose to allow the situation and issue to control us and make us a victim, or we can choose to shift our perspective from fear to empowered. If we are interpreting the issue as negative and threatening to our person or the relationship, it is because we gave it that meaning. (Again, abusive situations require your safety before working the issue) The good news is that if we made it volatile, we can also make it peaceful and workable. We can calm our feelings around it and approach the issue with calmness and wisdom.

This chapter is not about avoiding a relationship because of the additional issues involved. It is not to say that relationships are full of issues that need to be dealt with. It is not to say all the issues will be a painful and difficult.

On the contrary, most of the time, when approached with an open mind, the issues can add depth and width to the journey that is the relationship. When seen without judgment, the issues we will see, whether perceived as positive or negative, can be tiny little journeys within the overall journey we experience with our partners. Issues are not something to avoid, they are things to embrace and deal with together.

This chapter is simply a reminder to deal with the issues and continue loving your partner. Be a resource to each other and allow the issues to strengthen your bond, your love and your relationship. Allow the energy given to an issue to be neutral. It is at this point the issue can be dealt with lovingly and intelligently. It can be embraced by love and peace. The relationship wins, your partner wins and you win.

Create Safe Space –

Use Feedback to Claim Rather than Blame

A relationship is entered into by two people who love each other. Once the relationship comes to a certain point in its journey, vows are usually made that include things like sticking together through sickness and health, rich times and poor, good times and bad. Consider adding to your vows, either during the ceremony or as an addendum to your original vows, keep safe. If you are not married but still find yourself in a committed relationship, make this part of your agreement, understanding and commitment to each other.

Keeping safe carries with it several meanings, all of which are important. We, and our partner, both deserve the chance to have a safe zone in life. Where better to find that place than in the midst of our relationship and our own home.

For most of us, we would naturally act in defense of our partner when they face physical harm. Even if there is nothing we can do physically, our hearts and desires lead us to take some action to protect them. We find ourselves physically pained when there is nothing we can do for them as we truly want to ease their discomfort and keep them safe.

72

When we find them in pain and we have no resources to physically assist them, we can be strong for them. We can support them and help them in seeing the beauty of their heart, the strength of their resolve. We can demonstrate to them the power of our connection and the love we have to offer. We do not necessarily have to speak these words; actions say more anyway.

Keeping our relationships in the safe zone also includes causing no physical pain. Not only do we want to make sure no harmful outside experience occurs, we vow to not cause harm within the relationship. The physical abuse suffered in some relationships does not have to be. There are many resources for the abused as well as the abuser. Seek out those resources, swallow your pride and embrace the help and connection you will find.

If you are the abuser, be strong enough to say NO MORE! Stand up with your strength and refuse to cave into the immature tendencies that cause you to physically lash out. Stop the damage before it is too late for those you claim to love and for yourself as well. Allowing the manifestation of these tendencies to continue will create a habitual rage that will be increasingly more difficult to handle.

If you are the abused, stand up for you. Standing up for you may come in the form of standing your ground and not taking it anymore. It may mean walking out and finding shelter somewhere. It may mean not ever going back until major change has been proven.

As destructive as physical abuse is to a person and relationship. the most common way safety becomes an issue is when the emotional and mental safety of either person is overlooked. Comments causing pain are not always obvious and great care must be taken to remove these from the conversations. This is not to say we have to keep our mouths shut and never speak what is on our minds and hearts. Later in this chapter we will talk about a tool that allows us to speak up in a healthy and safe way.

Cute little jabs and intended jokes are often felt as strongly as poison darts, be careful. What we may think is a joke may actually be perceived as a verbal slap to our partner. If we have been in the relationship a long time, these things may be going on and we have no idea the depth of pain they cause. When we take a moment to consider our comments before speaking, we can ask ourselves, "Will these words cause pain?" If so, do not speak them.

These so-called innocent comments and jabs may have been going on so long that the sender and the receiver do not even realize how much hurt is being caused. The intention of these comments may have been a little fun. The sender may truly not know the impact of the comments.

The receiver may have become numb to them over the years. Numbness is near to lifeless. Being numb is worse than being hurt because at least being in pain is a sign of life. Being numb to feelings cheats us of living. While the feelings in these instances may be less than pleasant, the experience can lead us to some wonderful awareness and growth. The numbing cheats us of those opportunities.

Be considerate of your partner and open to your own feelings. Keep safe and allow love and well-being to guide your words and actions.

One of the most vital resources we have that assists us in elevating our relationships or expanding our lives in general is communications. Communication is a very broad topic and this book will present several key communication tools that coincide with the journey of life and relationship.

Use Feedback to Claim Rather than Blame is the first of the communication tools presented in this book. This tool allows us to keep ourselves and our partners safe and still be able to have conversations around touchy subjects.

Open and honest communication is key to creating a safe place for both of you. Speaking up when something has said or done something that emotionally cuts us is important to open the doors to healing.

Many of us tend to ignore or tune out hurtful words and actions in hopes that the situation will resolve itself. We may experience a brief relief by ignoring the subject, however, this can lead to deeper issues, like resentment and anger, if left unresolved. In other words, the hurtful situation will not heal itself on its own.

Ignoring and tuning out only lead to assumptions and these are usually based on comparisons or judgments we make. These comparisons and judgments are based on our past experiences and they tend to contribute to an unsafe environment within the relationship. It is in expressing our feelings that progress is made to understand, heal and resolve.

The problem with expressing our feelings is that we often fall into victim mode and forfeit our power. We express our feelings as something that occurred because of the action and words from our partner. We blame them for the feelings we have. We make statements like, "You did/said this, and it made me feel this." This is not authentic communication and will never lead to healing. In doing this, we claim that their actions and words have the power to make us feel a certain way.

Before moving out of this mindset, we must understand one thing; no one can make us feel anything. This does not mean that we do not feel hurt or happy, fearful of loving, chaotic or peaceful when something is said. It does not mean we are immune to feelings that arise from actions taken. It simply means, we choose the feelings we have based on things that were said and done.

As a society, we have decided that we must watch every word that comes out of our mouths, so we do not hurt someone. We have decided that we must reign in our actions so people around us are not uncomfortable. We are taught that we are responsible for other people's feelings. On the flip side, we are becoming thin skinned and feel others should be wary not to hurt us. If they do, it is all their fault.

It is time we take responsibility for our feelings and our holdbacks. We must begin again to express our feelings and thoughts without fear of what others think. Now, to do this, we must own those feelings and thoughts, especially in our relationship.

When we own our feelings and set aside the excuses and blaming, we empower ourselves to heal. We claim our power and seek truth. When something hurtful is said, we no longer have to hide from the feelings and we no longer need to cast blame. We can own it and express it in a positive, loving and healthy way. We can use feedback to claim rather than blame.

When we claim, we are not blaming. This is not suggesting that we claim full responsibility for what was said or done, just our reaction to it. We are only claiming the feelings we took on as a result of hurtful words or actions.

Doing this may sound similar to this, "When this happened, I felt this." We are not forfeiting our power, we are empowering ourselves. We are speaking to the issues without blaming. We are standing in our truth without attacking our partner.

The union that is the relationship, our partner and ourselves deserve the right to be safe and we deserve the right to be ourselves; our authentic selves. When we express as our true selves, from our essence, from our heart, we deliver no harm. When we come from this place of love that is within, we create and provide safety for ourselves, our partner and our relationship. We make space, both physical and emotional, where we love to be, and this space resonates for our partner to cherish as well.

Earlier, I mentioned Holdbacks. This brings us to another invaluable communication tool which walks hand in hand with "Use Feedback to Claim Rather than Blame." This tool is **"Take Responsibility for Your Holdbacks."**

This is very similar to the Feedback tool in that we are taking responsibility for the feelings we have and our part in the situation. The difference is that with the feedback tool, we are addressing things that happen outside of us and our reaction to those things. With **"Take Responsibility for Your Holdbacks,"** we are addressing what is going on inside of us. A holdback is something we carry inside and is driven by resentments, jealousy, anger and any other negative emotion. A holdback is just as it sounds; it is withholding love by carrying the burden of negativity.

Allowing a holdback to continue is even more damaging on the personal level than the blaming we use when lashing out at someone. In lashing out, the issues are at least brought to the surface and can usually be healed. A holdback is an internal behavior and we tend to cover them with a false smile, an "everything is alright" attitude and many other facades that show happiness but fail to reveal the true feelings beneath.

Years ago, and on many occasions since, I would frequently go to a historic street near where I lived. The street was home to many excellent restaurants, unique clubs, fascinating museums and some of the best music venues I could ever dream of. The buildings along the street were beautiful and along with the other offerings along the street, I could imagine what life would have been like years ago when the street was new. Many years after I began my visits to this wonderful place, the city's building inspectors discovered that behind the beautiful facades were buildings that were crumbling. As beautiful as it was to walk along the street, it was all about to collapse.

The same is true for us when we continually hold onto our holdbacks. We are putting a coat of paint on a deteriorating wall. The existence of the holdback is slowly eating away at our demeanor, our attitude, our positive outlook on life. A holdback slowly creates grander illusions that we are not worthy or good enough; our self-esteem crumbles little by little until there is nothing left to support the façade; then all falls.

To renovate the wholeness within ourselves and our relationships, we must heal what is behind the façade. Continually applying quick fixes to the façade so the exterior looks good only distracts us from dealing with the inner struggles and deterioration brought on by the holdbacks. We must wholly heal all parts of us, beginning with our hearts.

We heal by taking responsibility for our holdbacks and forgiving; forgiving ourselves, our partners and the circumstances that led to the holdbacks. The first step in taking responsibility for our holdbacks is to realize the holdbacks are of our own creation. No person, no action, no words, no situation can force us to take a holdback and call it our own. We create them. Granted, we create them based on what we have learned in the past, but that is merely an excuse. Holdbacks are a silent way to blame others for something that we felt.

The healing process for holdbacks begins with communications. When we first communicate with ourselves the truth of the holdback, claim our part in it and take responsibility, we have taken a huge step. Even though it is a huge step, it is still the first step. From this first step we seek understanding as to why this holdback developed within us. We must identify the lessons we are to learn from this holdback. Holdbacks are not to be ignored; we do not just step around them and act as if they do not exist, we face them and find understanding. When we are clear about the reasons the holdback developed and what we can learn, we can release it and forgive ourselves for allowing it to remain for however long it was within. Since the holdback is completely of our making, we can choose how best to release and forgive.

If the holdback we carry is aimed at another person; we can forgive the words or actions that invited us to develop the holdback. We silently forgive this person and release them from the responsibility of the holdback. They did not create it; we did. We may want to carry on a conversation with the other person and clear the air. We must remember though; the other person may not even be aware of the holdback. If we did not bring the holdback to their attention, they may be oblivious to it.

The communication in this tool is primarily about the conversation between our head, which made up the holdback, and our heart, the feeling and forgiving center of our being. This balance between our minds and our hearts is

79

wholeheartedness. When we wholeheartedly open communications, awareness and understanding, we see truth and when the light of truth is shined on any holdback, we will see it shrinking and ultimately disappearing. Whether we speak this release to the other person or persons involved or keep it within ourselves, healing occurs.

Take Responsibility for Your Holdbacks. It is a cleansing, a healing, a re-building. Clear your heart and mind of all that holds you back and experience a fresh new outlook on life, relationship, your partner and yourself.

Work Together

Explore Joint Decisions

Many of us in committed relationships know the importance of working together on the big decisions. Buying a new house, vehicles or raising children usually entail input from both partners and the importance of working together is obvious.

There are many other decisions that affect the relationship or the people in it and these too merit consideration by all parties. If the decision to do or not do something touches the life of either partner, it is best addressed as a joint decision. If the results of the decision effects the time spent at home or away from home, it is best addressed as a joint decision. If the result of the decision monetarily affects the relationship, it is best addressed as a joint decision. In other words, every choice that we can make that affects our partner or our relationship is best addressed as a joint decision. And in truth, most decisions, even those seemingly inconsequential ones, affect the relationship in some fashion.

Consideration for our partner is vital if we desire a relationship that works. No matter how much we may think a decision will touch only our life, our partner and the relationship are likely to be affected by it as well. It may seem that a decision only affects our attitude, our well-being, our demeanor and other things that are personal and internal, however, what affects us also affects our expression and our expression directly affects those around us, as well.

When we choose to enter into a relationship, we are no longer alone anymore. Any attempt to trick ourselves into thinking we are, is an illusion. We decided at some point that we wanted to be in a relationship and have a partner. It is important to remember that partners are not just for the bedroom, they are for all of life. Most of us entered into a relationship based on the love we had for our partner and our partner most likely did the same. With this commitment to each other, everything we do affects them and everything they do affects us. We are now partners in all things.

Working together is not reserved for the "BIG" decisions. Our relationship, our partner and ourselves are best served when all decisions, great and small, become a joint decision. Even in those times when the choice truly does fall to us, the inclusion or our partner in the decision-making process strengthens our connection.

When we recognize our partner as a valuable ally and resource who has our best interest at heart, we can hear their thoughts and ideas and more openly consider what it is we are seeking to decide. When we consider their opinions, we expand our awareness and often transform our original thoughts on a subject to something better than we could ever realize alone.

When we tap into our partner's knowledge, open awareness to their concerns and embrace their desire for our best interest, we elevate our ability to make decisions that serve all.

Your Beliefs Create Your Reality

Henry Ford once said, "If you think you can do a thing or think you can't do a thing, you're right." This is one of the most powerful and true statements I have ever heard.

Our thoughts determine our experience of life. What we think becomes what we feel. What we feel becomes energy. Our energy determines our action. And, our action creates our reality; our experience.

The power of our beliefs is astounding. In each of the group events I facilitate, I demonstrate the power of our thoughts and beliefs. I ask for a volunteer from the group who believes they have good upper body strength. I have this person stand at the front of the room facing away from the audience and in a place where they cannot see a flip chart that I use for the process.

I ask the group to remain silent throughout the demonstration and then write on the flip chart, "You are Weak and Worthless". Remember the volunteer cannot see this. I ask the group to believe this about the volunteer. I encourage, for a moment, to believe that this is the truth of this person. I then ask the person to raise their arms out to their side and resist me with all their strength as I attempt to pull their dominant arm down to their side. I can immediately, with little or no effort at all, move their arm completely to their side.

I then ask the volunteer to relax and shake off what just occurred while I have the group erase those thoughts from their mind. We all take a deep breath and we move to step two of this demonstration. I now write "You are Strong and Worthy" on the chart and ask the group to believe this about the volunteer. Once the group has had a chance to begin believing this, I ask the volunteer to raise their arms again as I attempt to pull their arm to their side.

This time, their arm will move very little, if at all; never have I been able to take their arm all the way to their side as I did in the other portion of the demonstration. Many times, their arm will not waver at all. I have done this in reverse order and get the same results every time. I have done this demonstration so many times I have lost count, and it has never failed. The group's beliefs are strong enough to create someone else's reality. So, what are our beliefs creating within us, our partner and our relationship?

Another powerful demonstration of this truth is found in a study from the late 1980s about prayer a teacher once told me about. In a study of 400 patients with similar illness and identical treatments, a group of fifty people were brought in to pray affirmative prayer for half the group. The people praying were asked to pray to whatever they believed was their highest power; God, Allah, Jesus, Buddha, Universe, Highest good, etc. The people were praying for two hundred patients and were not made aware of the other two hundred. None of the patients were told of this experiment. The affirmative prayers were focused on healing for the two hundred patients.

Within the pre-determined time period, the two hundred patients that had been prayed for showed nearly an eighty percent greater rate of healing than the two hundred patients who received no prayer from the group.

Affirmative prayer is speaking beliefs about something. It is holding that which is being prayed for in positive light. Affirmative prayer is belief and beliefs create reality.

(My search for the origins of this study failed and the teacher, a practicing psychiatrist for 32 years, who told me of it, could not remember where she read it other than one of her medical journals. In my search, I found as many studies from that time period claiming prayer has no affect as I did those claiming it does have an effect. More recent studies seem to be trending towards supporting the power of prayer.)

Whether it be prayer, thinking, or belief, our mental, emotional and spiritual energy carry power. With that kind of power, what are our thoughts and beliefs creating in our relationship? What are we creating in our partner? What are we creating in ourselves? What we believe about our partner will determine what type of partner we will have. If we believe our partner is a jerk, guess what our partner will be. If we believe them to be loving and kind, guess what they will be.

A wonderful post that has made its way around social media reads, "Don't believe everything you think." Our minds play many tricks on us when we are not connected to our truth or expressing from love. Ego sets in and convinces us of many un-truths about ourselves, our partners and everyone else in our lives. We make up all kinds of stuff while ego is in charge. Truth is found when we connect through our heart and see with loving eyes.

We are greatly served when we consider our beliefs and transform any that are not serving our greatest good.

When we shift our beliefs, we shift our experience of both life and relationship.

Create the reality you desire by believing good, love, peace.

Start Where You Are

Notice what is working

Get to Know Each Other Again

Getting to know each other again is about reconnecting with our partner on the deepest levels of love. With this tool, we are opening awareness to the beliefs and perceptions we have formed as we spent time with our partner. As time moves on, we create beliefs, assumptions, and judgments about our partners. Some of these beliefs serve the relationship well and others do not. This tool is about understanding our beliefs and letting go of all that do not serve the relationship. If a belief does not elevate and expand love in the relationship, it does not deserve to remain in our thoughts. This tool is about seeing our partner in a new light. It is about seeing beyond those limiting beliefs and seeing our partner's authentic essence, their true self.

When we limit ourselves to see only the façade they show, we are not seeing the authenticity of our partner. When we believe what we have made up about our partner due to their egoic self and behaviors, we are cheating ourselves and our partner of the truth that is available. We often get hung up in seeing only the part of them that rises to the surface in difficult situations and we often miss their heart.

Remember back when you first fell in love and began the relationship? You saw much more of their essence than their ego. In fact, the love you had for them may have blinded you to their ego completely.

The love we feel for our partner allows us to see their authentic self. The love we express to them allows them to see our essence, our authenticity. As we hold them in love, our entire environment becomes more loving.

Unfortunately, unless we have done in depth work on living fully in our authenticity, over time essence gives way to ego. Chances are, as the passion of the relationship faded, or even stopped, so did the frequency of times we saw the essence of our partner or expressed our own essence.

As life together settled into routines, we may have experienced the daily fire of passion becoming more of a spark instead of that roaring blaze we once saw. As time went on, the passion that flamed in our relationship may have become a rare occurrence at best. We sometimes find the authentic part of our partner and ourselves becoming harder to notice. Our egos tend to take more control than our essences, and we began to see more negative traits than positive in both of us and the relationship itself.

Over time we develop beliefs, perceptions, judgments and opinions about our partner, as they do for us. Some of these may have factual data to back them up, and our beliefs may be founded in truth. Other beliefs may be built on assumptions we made along the way and have no support from facts or truth. Even those beliefs that are built on fact may be totally in the past and absolutely not relevant today, yet we keep hanging on.

Even the accurate perceptions, those that do remain true, can harm the relationship because holding tightly to any belief, limits the possibility of growth for ourselves, our partner and the relationship. When we only see negative in a person or situation, negative is all that can come of that person or situation. Our beliefs not only create our reality, they will heavily influence, if not totally create, our partner's reality, as well.

Turning off any beliefs that do not support the highest good that we can imagine for our relationship opens us, our partner and our relationship to amazing growth.

Getting to know our partner and ourselves again will challenge our belief system. While many of us may not want to challenge what we "know" to be true, it is necessary if we want to raise the beauty, wonder and love in the relationship. Elevating our relationship will never occur by holding on to the same energy and beliefs that created our current situation. Whether we are living in an amazing relationship or a struggling one, we can elevate and expand the love. We must to do something different to achieve different results.

As we consider our beliefs, we must be careful not to judge them as wrong, bad or broken. We are simply considering what is working to elevate our relationship and what is not working. When we fail to elevate our relationship to new levels, stagnation sets in and life can easily become dull, passion fades and love becomes difficult to realize.

"Getting to Know Each Other Again" is an invitation to see your partner and yourself as you did when the love and passion was at its strongest. You can rekindle the sparks of passion, and those sparks can again become flames. This consideration of your thoughts and beliefs is not an opportunity to dig up more dirt on yourself or your partners. It is an opportunity to reignite the fires of love that once burned so brightly.

Turning again to the flames of passion, we allow the love we find to be our guide to elevating the relationship. Once love is the light through which we see our partners, ourselves and the relationship, we have a foundation, a guiding light, to consider the beliefs we carry. From this place of love, we can look at each belief and perception and ask ourselves, "Is this really True?" In this action we release assumptions, and we let go of all we made up. We can begin to consider if any good can come from this belief or if we need to release it completely. Through this light of love, we can entertain the possibilities available for growth and learning

Our relationship is a journey. We are constantly evolving along this journey and so is our partner. Each day is a wonderful opportunity to learn something new about ourselves and our partner and when we can adopt this mindset, we get to know each other again, every day. With this mindset, passion elevates and expands beyond all we could ever imagine.

Recognize What Is Working

     Many of us tend to focus on what needs to change, what is not working, and what causes pain and suffering in our relationships and lives. We can see evidence of this by simply turning on the nightly news. The news media has become one of the largest industries in the world by showing us negative stories each day, all day. We have been taught that focusing on all that is wrong is how we figure out how to "fix" those things. Focusing on the negative will never "fix" it. Sure, we must recognize what is not working before we transform that thing into something that serves our highest good; however, focusing on the negative usually leads us to sinking further into judgement, comparison and other negative energetic feelings.

     When we focus on the negative, we add more negativity into the beliefs and behaviors associated with the situation. Focusing on the negative of a situation fuels the negativity of the situation. Expressing positive energy brings the situation out of the darkness of negativity and into the light. We transform the situation from fear to love. To change anything, we must change our thoughts about that thing.

     Our thoughts become our energy, our energy becomes our beliefs, our beliefs determine our actions and our actions become our realities. This chapter is about seeing what is working in the relationship, in our partners and in ourselves. When we turn our focus to what works, we empower what we see, and we attract more that works.

Focusing on what works in the relationship allows us to see hope; hope of love and hope for elevating and expanding our relationship. Many of us have done this on occasion, yet nothing changed. We may have seen a spark of positivity in the growth of our relationship only to quickly find ourselves right back where we were yesterday.

Recognizing what is working is not a once and done thing. It is a new behavior we adopt and practice daily, multiple times a day. Recognizing what is working is easy to do, not so easy to remember to do. Some great ways to remind ourselves to seek the positive include placing notes on mirrors, in our cars, on our computer monitor; setting an alert on our phones; making a note in our calendars. To create new habits and behaviors, we must remind ourselves to put into practice a behavior that encourages us to move towards that which we desire.

We must continually look for the positive things in our partners, relationship and self. We must look for them, embrace them and be grateful for them. In gratitude and appreciation, we create a positive energy that attracts more we can hold in gratitude.

Judgments, Comparisons, expectations and the "should" mentality will come back into our lives even when we turn our focus and attention to the positive. Even though we may be seeking the positive nature of our partners, if they are not using these tools with us, their behaviors will be slow to change and when our attention comes to rest on the lack of change, we will be invited to turn our focus more deeply to that lack of change; we will more easily tune into the negativity.

When we turn our focus to the positive in our partners, when we see them through eyes of love, we will see flickers of positive light. The mindful awareness of our feelings will alert us as to where our attention lies. When we feel down or negative, we are focused on the negative. When we feel happy and light, we are focused on the positive.

Alright, back to our tool. "Embrace What Is Working." What feels to be on track? What is elevating your relationship? What feels good about you and your partner and your relationship?

As you look at what is working, recognize the feelings you have while experiencing the things you recognize. Do you feel loved, happy, comforted, peaceful or is it something else? Does this feeling resonate with your heart? Is this something you want to increase? Are there other areas of your relationship that give you the same feelings?

Creating a mental or written check list of all that is working well in our relationships, we can tune into the feelings associated with those things more frequently. Allowing these feelings to fill our hearts and become our focus, we soon find more of those feelings when we see our partners, our relationships and life. Energies attract like energy; when our energy is loving and peaceful, we will experience more love and peace.

Many of us put so much importance on fixing what is not working that we ignore what is working well. We focus on the feelings associated with the "not working" things and fail to realize the love and peace that may fill every other area of the relationship. It is similar to the old black and white cartoon where the old crow was so intent on cutting off the dead tree limb, he did not notice he was sitting on the part that would fall to the ground.

Granted, those things that are not working may deserve some attention and direction, but to give them the entirety of our attention and focus cheats us from realizing and experiencing the wonderful moments, the loving glances and the offered embrace. Giving all our attention to the things that are not working attract more of the same into our relationship.

Feel the feelings, open awareness to the beauty and love of the relationship and experience all that is working. As awareness opens and loving feelings are revealed, embrace them and allow them to resonate from within. Embrace all that is working.

Give Your 100%

In every moment of our lives we have an opportunity to give one hundred percent. Unfortunately, in our fast-paced world there seems to be little or no time to give it. We are tempted to cut corners and do just enough to get on to the next project. We are encouraged to get things done as fast as possible even though the quality and our experience of that thing is diminished. We often hold back our one hundred percent and wait for others to step up and give theirs. We sometimes fail to give our one hundred percent when we convince ourselves that our best is not good enough.

In relationships, whether intimate or social, we fall into the belief that the relationship is 50/50 with the other person, but that could not be further from the truth.

Giving one hundred percent does not mean that we must give more than we have to offer. It is not about struggling until we have nothing left. Giving one hundred percent does not mean we must sacrifice every waking moment to a project or someone else. Think about that for a moment: when we are giving so much of ourselves to a project or person that we have no time to slow down and experience what we are doing, when we are so focused on just getting it done, we have no time to embrace and enjoy the process. We often fall into resentment and anger and this leads us further from what one hundred percent truly can be. Giving one hundred percent does not mean we must do things the same way, with the same effort, as someone else. We define our own one hundred percent. Our one hundred percent fluctuates, and it is authentic to each of us. We will talk about more about this in a bit.

Withholding our one hundred percent cheats us from expressing as the incredible beings we truly are. Withholding our one hundred percent cheats us out of experiencing the project and the person as our authentic selves. Seeing ourselves as limited humans cheats us and the world out of the dynamic, creative, amazing beings that we are.

In truth, we are spiritual beings having an amazing human experience. We have much more to offer than the things we can do. There is more within us to share than what is confined within this human shell. When we rely on our humanness to dictate and direct what we do in life, we are not giving the intangible aspect of our truth; we are not giving one hundred percent of who we are.

One of the key ingredients to giving our one hundred percent is experiencing and expressing from our hearts, our spiritual selves. Our expression and awareness of our authenticity in all we do is as much a part of giving one hundred percent as the physical things we do. We are capable of completely transforming our relationships and our lives by including our hearts more deeply than the occasional mention of "I Love You."

We put ourselves in a vulnerable position when we express from this deeper place within our essence. Vulnerability, however, is not the weakness we have come to believe. Vulnerability is one of our greatest strengths and resources in relationships and throughout life. When we allow vulnerability, we release the judgments of how things "should" be and open ourselves to how things "can" be. We realize a deeper love within us and around us. Through vulnerability, we express more authentically and gift ourselves and others with the truth that lies within. When we embrace vulnerability, when we express and experience this deeper love as the ultimate gift that it is, we open understanding of what is truly important.

We have many things in this world feeding the belief that we should only give as much as we receive. Society is quickly taking on an "every person for themselves" mentality. Examples of the, "Get them before they get me," behavior are found nearly everywhere we look. In these mind-sets, we are invited to see lack in every situation. We have come to believe that if we do not "get ours" first, there will not be enough left over for us. This comes into play with everything from monetary and material things to emotional availability.

People all around us are airing their gripes about giving more to the relationship than the other people involved. We see this behavior on social media, television and our friends and family. When we open awareness to our own behaviors, we are likely to find that we, too, have a gripe or two. We often feel this way in our relationships as well as our personal and business life. I see examples of this in my individual coaching, my group coaching and my corporate training events.

When these beliefs are present in our thought process, we are focusing on what others are doing, or not doing. It is easy to perceive the other person is not trying as hard or giving as much. We feel discouraged and soon may begin to feel as though we are wasting our efforts. When this perception takes over, we stop giving our own one hundred percent and allow the actions of others to determine how we define our experience.

It does not matter if the relationship is of an intimate or business nature, a family member or a friend. When we begin comparing our efforts to theirs, we disempower ourselves and the situation. Our relationship falters and can easily deteriorate. This external focus takes away from our ability to authentically give our one hundred percent in the situation. The simple act of focusing on what others are doing prevents us from giving what we truly have within ourselves to give.

We have all been in a relationship with someone else, whether it be for a moment in passing or years long. We have all felt in one or more relationships that we are giving more, and if we are honest with ourselves, we may feel we gave less. Either way, we are comparing and judging. Even if these feelings are founded on truth, they do not serve the relationship, the desired results of the relationship or ourselves when we hold onto this comparison; this focus. Holding on to comparing and judging decreases our ability to give the fullness of our authenticity and love. In our comparisons and judgments, we cripple our own expression of love; we stifle the goodness we can send out into the world and we drastically limit the goodness and love we receive.

We must silence that nagging voice inside our head that compares. This is ego and it will quickly begin telling us that the other person in this relationship does not care as much. It will tell us that we do not deserve to have the results the relationship has to offer. Ego will tell us that the success of the relationship is reliant on the other person's input and it will tell us to just stop trying if they are not willing to up their game. The ego carries us into victim mode and tells us we are at the mercy of other people's actions. Many relationships end for this very reason.

When we buy into the belief that all must be equal, and allow it to continue, we often come to a point where frustration sets in and we shut down our efforts and wait for the other person to begin giving as much as we do. All is not equal, and it never will be and that can be an invaluable gift. We are all unique individuals bringing our own experiences, knowledge and gifts into the relationship. We cannot be equal unless we give up our uniqueness and that would be quite boring and sad. Giving up uniqueness cheats our partners, our relationships and ourselves out of truth and possibility.

Equality is not to be completely avoided in relationships. Creating opportunities to express deeper love is an example of how equality can serve relationships. Fully respecting and valuing self and others and choosing to be happy is yet another example. However, due to the authentic uniqueness of every individual, we set ourselves up for disappointment if we believe our partner should act and be just like us.

When we adopt the need for sameness over authenticity, we easily turn our focus to differences and define them as bad or wrong, and we often find ourselves shutting down our efforts into the relationship. Shutting down only creates more tension and friction. Most of the time, our partner will have no clue that we feel this way, and they may begin wondering why we are not giving one hundred percent, and they in turn begin to shut down even further. We are the authors of our own vicious cycles.

The vicious cycle brings us back to the fifty/fifty thinking which is a relationship killer. The truth is, relationships, or anything you committed to in life, require one hundred percent from you. We can always hope to see our partners giving one hundred percent; however, the comparison and judgment we use to determine their level of participation prevents us from giving our own fullness. When we are not giving our own one hundred percent, we will never experience that which we desire.

When we give anything less than our completeness, the experience of the relationship is hard. When we are struggling, we are not giving one hundred percent. On the opposite side of this scenario, when we do give one hundred percent, our experience of the relationship or project flows and seems effortless; it is easy. Even in those situations where other people involved are not giving fully, when we do, our experience will feel easy and flowing.

When we are giving one hundred percent, but our partner is not, we serve ourselves, our partner and our relationship well when we keep giving it. When we give our authentic self, which is always one hundred percent, we give love; we are lifting the entire relationship. When we are fully authentic and give one hundred percent, we may see our partner being lifted emotionally, and they may begin giving a little more. Even if they do not, when we continue offering our all, we are honoring ourselves and the authentic part of the relationship. When we live, express and experience through our amazing truth, we radiate peaceful light and love over all.

Now, this does not mean we must become a caretaker for our partner; we do not serve ourselves or the relationship when we attempt to do more than our share. When we become caretaker for someone who is physically, mentally and emotionally able to care for themselves, we enable them to continue giving only a small percentage of themselves into the relationship. Giving one hundred percent includes caring for our own well-being. Part of caring for self is giving our partners space to grow, learn and stand in their own authenticity.

Giving one hundred percent is standing up for what we believe; it is sticking to our values and morals. Giving our one hundred percent includes expressing our feelings and communicating our views, with love. Giving one hundred percent is being the best and most authentic person we can be throughout life and the relationships. As we express our authenticity, we give our partners the gift of seeing us at our strongest and our weakest. Giving one hundred percent is expressing authentically each day, and it is giving the same opportunity to our partners without judgment or comparison.

To further demonstrate the importance of giving one hundred percent, here are some interesting statistics that would develop if 99.9% were attained instead of one hundred percent.

For these stats, let's assume that 99.9% was good enough. If so,

> ➤ More than 4,000 newborn babies would be sent home with the wrong parents this year
> ➤ More than 400,000 mismatched pairs of shoes will be shipped this week
> ➤ More than 15,000 books will be shipped with the wrong covers this week
> ➤ This week, 80,000 incorrect drug prescriptions will be written
> ➤ With just one of the most popular credit cards, more than 900,000 credit cards in circulation will have incorrect user information on the magnetic strips
> ➤ More than 10,000,000 income tax returns will be incorrectly processed this year

- More than 500 coronary bypass procedures will fail by the end of the year
- More than 650 ATMs will dispense the wrong amount of cash in the next hour in the United States alone.
- 102 airline flights per day will not land safely

These numbers are not given to indicate that these industries are making these types of mistakes. They may be doing better, maybe not. The numbers are simply to demonstrate how 99.9% is not good enough. The same goes for us in our relationships and all of life, as well. Giving less than one hundred percent of our authentic selves jeopardizes the success of anything we attempt including our relationships, our projects and our own happiness.

The failure rate of diets or exercise programs are other great examples of not giving one hundred percent. People begin diets every day. The diet industry is one of the largest on this planet. Some people have great success on their diets while others, no matter how much effort they exert, simply cannot lose the weight they want lose. We blame these results on metabolism or glands or hormones. While there is some truth to that, not giving one hundred percent is usually the culprit. I can speak to this as I have been one of those who has tried and not succeeded as I would have liked.

Giving one hundred percent to the diet and/or exercise goes far beyond what we put in our mouths or put our bodies through in the gym. To give one hundred percent in this scenario, we must incorporate diet and exercise. We must transform our mindset and lifestyle. We must embrace the entire journey. Giving one hundred percent is merging our emotional and spiritual self with our mental and physical self. Giving one hundred percent is bringing all aspects of ourselves to the party.

Obviously, when we set our intentions to a project or relationship, there are instances where physical effort can be used to move things along. However, if we do things just to stay busy and create the illusion of progress, we miss an opportunity to experience the authentic journey. We become focused on the future instead of the present moment. In focusing on the future, we face another element of life that pulls us further away from giving our one hundred percent; FEAR.

One of my favorite definitions of **FEAR** is <u>F</u>uture <u>E</u>vents <u>A</u>ppearing <u>R</u>eal. Even if that which we are working towards is awesome, when we do not focus on present moment, we chance missing a beautiful experience, and we find fear standing in our path along with all kinds of things to worry about. A shift in thinking and focus will open us to giving one hundred percent.

Anytime we are not in the flow, fear is present. It may not be one of the paralyzing moments most of us define as fear, however, it is present. Hesitation to change, a thought that does not resonate with our intentions, judgment and comparisons are all byproducts of fear. Fear is any ego driven thought or feeling that tempts us to hold back from revealing our wholeness. Fear invites us to hold something of ourselves in reserve in case things do not work out as planned.

Fear does present itself throughout life, however, we choose our experience of it. We can allow it to cast a dark shadow over our experience or we can seek learning and meaning from it. We can face it and step through the fear to the intentions we have for any situation or relationship. Each of us is able to re-direct our experience, and we can move

104

from fear to joy quickly. It is a conscious choice we can make to turn to our truth.

Now, giving our one hundred percent does not mean we are always giving and never receiving. It is not about giving all of ourselves until we have nothing left to give; that serves no one. In our intimate relationship for instance, when we tend only to our partner's needs and ignore our own, we are not serving the greatest good of the relationship, our partner or self. There are times when we may need to tend to our partner's needs. We must be sure, though, to not ignore our own needs in the process.

Here are some things to remember about giving one hundred percent.

First, giving your one hundred percent is not completely about effort. While there may be some physical things we can do to more fully give our all in the relationship, giving one hundred percent is more about seeing our partner, the relationship and ourselves through eyes of pure love. Sometimes infusing a situation with the energy of peace is giving one hundred percent. When we are constantly moving and doing and thinking, we are missing out on the experience and the expression available to us and to the situation.

Next, it is vital to understand that everyone's one hundred percent is different. We all express one hundred percent differently and it fluctuates. Our one hundred percent, and the other person's, will vary depending on how we feel. When we are feeling on top of the world, our experience and expression of one hundred percent will be at one level. When we are tired, hungry, sad, angry or just in a funk, our one hundred percent will be exhibited and experienced at a lower level.

Just know this; the down days are not cause to beat ourselves up. And, we must remember to not be hard on our partners for the same reason. If we are having fun with a project or person, our one hundred percent will be much higher than if we are dreading the project or bored with it.

We have all heard the interviews after big games with athletes and coaches where they claim to have given 110%. Many of us have wondered how to get to that level. Well, we cannot, and neither can they. There is no such thing as 110% effort. One hundred percent is the best we can do, and it is perfect. These athletes simply experienced the adrenaline of the game, the excitement of the crowd, the focus of intention and those things motivated them to a higher level of one hundred percent than ordinary days. One hundred percent does grow as you do, and it is as fluid as you; it is ever changing.

Tuning into the positive energy, the love and the authenticity of ourselves and the relationship will lift our expression into the relationship and life. Creating an atmosphere of fun will move us beyond the fears of comparison and judgment and lift us to express more fully.

We serve ourselves well when we let go of judgment and comparison about the levels of participation and expression we or others are giving. When we can see the expression more than the lack in every situation and relationship, we can foster an environment inviting the authentic experience we desire. As mentioned earlier, our energetic expression, more than the words we say or the actions we take, dictates the feelings and environment around us. When we believe the other person to be slacking in the project or relationship, even if we keep our mouths shut, we create an energetic environment that the other person will detect. Our thoughts will transform the experience and energy for the good or the not so good and we get to choose between the two.

The best thing we can do in all situations is to give our one hundred percent. This comes from our heart more than our minds. When we lovingly and gratefully express as our authentic selves, when we turn our focus to what we are experiencing and leave comparison out of it, we can truly move into the flow of life that offers unlimited love and peace.

Tune in and be fully present emotionally, physically, mentally and spiritually. When everything is flowing and seems easy even in difficult times, we are at one hundred percent. If we are struggling, we are not quite there. One hundred percent is easy; 99.9% is difficult. This is not an indicator to get busier. In most cases, this simply means we are holding back some part of ourselves and are not fully participating from the heart. We can look within without judgment and take note of where we are withholding a part of ourselves.

Giving 100% is complete participation, expressing and experiencing, giving and receiving, without judging what we give. It is about giving fully from essence. It is about doing what we can do authentically no matter what the other person is doing or not doing.

Nurture You

In our intentions to elevate relationships or any other part of our lives, we tend to look outside of ourselves for the things we can do to improve things and make them a little better. Our thoughts turn outwardly in hopes of finding the quick fix or newest trend in relationships that will make everything perfect. It is not until our search leads us back into our authenticity, our hearts, that we will find what we seek.

Manifesting the results we desire is an inside job and we will never realize those results by looking out into the world for solutions. There are many programs that offer insight into ways to elevate our relationship. There are many books, this one for instance, that shed light on how to expand our relationships. There are wonderful examples in many areas of our lives that show how to take our relationships to the next level when we are open to see them, however, the answers that are perfectly aligned with our highest good and heartfelt desires are found within.

The things that occur around us, the books we read, the programs we attend and the other examples available to us may offer incredible insights and lessons, yet they do us no good if we do not bring them into our hearts and use them for ourselves first. Nothing will assist us in taking our relationships, or life in general, to elevated levels until we use the lessons and resources for ourselves internally, open awareness to them, learn and grow in our essence, and then express outwardly from our authentic selves.

We must release the victim mentality that tells us outside sources are responsible for our well-being. We must let go of the belief that our partner must change before we can realize the change we desire. We must release the belief that something outside of ourselves will fix or elevate us. We must become our own hero and we do that by taking responsibility for our own well-being and growth.

Turning our focus to our hearts, our highest self, we find that the solutions we seek and the answers we need are already present within. In our hearts, we find a connection to Universal wisdom, we find God, Highest Self, Light, Love; we find our Higher Power. To realize this most authentic connection and reveal the answers we seek, we must learn to nurture ourselves. In nurturing ourselves, we recognize and embrace our authenticity. We are not turning our backs on our partners or our relationships, we are simply turning our focus and awareness to that place within where we connect spiritually and emotionally with Source. In this inward look, we elevate our connection to others as well.

To fully nurture ourselves, we must recognize and embrace each component of our being; the physical, the mental, the emotional and the spiritual. A peaceful and flowing life experience is found when all components are in balance.

Most of us nurture one of the components; some of us may even nurture two. Complete balance in our life experience does not occur until we can bring each aspect of our being together in unity and it is then that our highest good is served. It is then that the highest good of our relationship and our partner is served.

To understand how we can more completely nurture ourselves, we must look at each component of our being individually before we can integrate them and nurture our whole self.

Nurturing Our Physical Self

The physical self is the most understood and usually receives the most attention. While not all the attention we give our bodies is healthy or beneficial, most of us have at least an idea of how to take care of our physical needs. For those things we do not know, there are thousands, if not millions, of resources we can tap into to find answers.

Leading the list of healthy ways to nurture our bodies are rest, nutrition and exercise.

In our fast-paced society, we tend to neglect rest. Most of us forfeit the rest we need for the things we feel we need to do. As our schedules become more full and hectic, we add more time to our day by resting less. When the stress and frustrations of our day grow into overwhelm, we tend to spend our sleep time worrying about how to make life come together. Even when we manifest something positive and beneficial into our lives, we tend to allow the excitement to steal time from the rest we need. As our lives become busier and more chaotic, we cheat ourselves of an important ingredient to successfully handling it all - rest.

Gifting more rest to ourselves, whether that be through sleep or mindful down-time, we gift ourselves clarity of thoughts. We gift ourselves the ability to organize the thoughts that are running through our heads and release those that hold no value for us. When we are rested, the overwhelm of fear does not present as strong.

When we are rested, our bodies are stronger. We heal during our moments of rest. Our immune systems become stronger when we rest, and a strong immune system is key to healing the struggles our bodies are facing. Of course, combined with good nutrition and exercise, we elevate our immune systems even more, however, rest is the first essential ingredient to nurturing our physical bodies.

Nutrition is vitally important as well. Proper nutrition gives our bodies the ingredients needed to work as designed. Giving our body the nutrients, vitamins and minerals that it needs promotes health and healing. We become stronger and again, we gain mental clarity as well.

Fabulous work is being done through nutrition to heal every disease, ailment and disorder imaginable. I have seen beautiful examples of people healing through nutrition. And, they are healing from much more than the common cold or allergies. While these are certainly part of the list, there is much more.

I have personally overcome shingles, diabetes and other ailments through nutrition. I have seen people healed of Lupus, heart disease, cancer and many other illnesses through nutrition as well.

Elevating our understanding of nutrition is key to healing and nurturing our physical bodies. Of course, a healthy diet is a wonderful place to start, however, there is much more we can do nutritionally to elevate our physical well-being.

Exercise is another of the key ingredients needed to nurture ourselves physically, and it goes far beyond building stronger muscles. Exercise creates an energy flow within that encourages healing and well-being.

When we exercise we must energize all parts of our physical bodies. People who visit a gym regularly speak of having leg days and arm days and chest days. This is a fabulous place to start and we must remember to bring in the cardio work and the flexibility exercises. It is movement of our entire bodies that benefit us the most.

There are many reasons to exercise; some of us want to be lean and fit, some want to live longer, some of us want to feel better. Each of these reasons is perfect. Whatever our reason, we must remember to find exercises that allow the flow of energy to circulate throughout the entirety of the body. It is this energetic flow that promotes healing and creates a foundation from which we elevate and expand our experience in this human vessel. All parts of our physical selves must be given the attention they deserve.

Of course, there are many ways to nurture our physical bodies and we must find what serves our greatest good. Massage, spas, dancing, walks in nature, bicycling, kayaking all come to mind and there is so much more. When we become curious and try new things, we will not only have the experience of the new practice, we will nurture different parts of our physical selves as well. Exercise does not have to be work or something we dread, it can be fun and exciting.

Nurturing Our Mental Self

We nurture ourselves on the mental level when we mind our thoughts. Our thoughts, more than any other thing, dictate our experience of life and our well-being. When our thoughts turn to judgments, comparison, expectations we easily move into dark and limiting thoughts. Nurturing ourselves mentally comes when we create new thoughts and beliefs that serve us.

We have between 50,000 and 80,000 thoughts per day, and the vast majority of these are happening in the sub-conscious. It is easy to tune into the thoughts playing in our conscious mind, only about ten percent; it is not so easy to recognize the other ninety percent. While it may not be easy, it is not impossible either.

112

These subconscious thoughts have accumulated over the years. We picked them up from our experiences and our attention to what other people in our lives did, said or experienced. Many of these thoughts have no value to us personally, however, they all have great impact on how we interpret and experience life. If for instance, we witnessed our mother being abused by our father, we can easily distrust and fear men. If we witnessed an abusive mother, we can easily distrust and fear women. If a bully was a predominate figure in our lives, we can easily distrust and fear anyone with an aggressive personality. If one of our closest friends portrayed a negativity towards religion, we can have a negative outlook on religions. The list can go on and on.

Our thoughts become judgments and create great generalizations and assumptions. Many, if not most, of these thoughts will not hold true when we open our awareness to them and recognize the truth, or lack of truth in them. It is in this recognition that we empower ourselves to release the thoughts that hold no truth or value for our current life experience.

Nurturing ourselves mentally begins with one question; "What am I thinking now?" When we ask this question and allow answers to come, we can recognize our thoughts and identify them as serving us or limiting us. We, alone, have the authority and the choice to change our thoughts. We can let go of the ones that hinder our experience of life and we can embrace the ones that lift us up. We can choose to bring light into our thinking or we can sink into the dark thoughts that tell us we are not good enough.

We nurture ourselves mentally when we choose light and goodness in our thoughts.

Nurturing Our Emotional Self

While emotions are true for us no matter what transpired to create them, we have a choice on which ones to embrace, which ones to transform and which to release. Even if there is no factual basis for the emotion we are feeling, the fact that we are feeling it makes it true in our experience of life. This does not mean we have to hold tight to it; we do not need to carry it with us for the rest of our lives. We can release or transform those emotions that hinder our life. We nurture ourselves when we shift from those emotions shrouded in darkness to positive and enlightening feelings.

When something "bad" happens, we have a choice; we can hold to the dark feelings surrounding the experience or we can turn our focus to the strength within that brought us through it. We can shift our perceptions of the situation and find goodness and we can allow that goodness to fill our being. In all situations, there is light, hope and love. The darkness we feel is the illusion that no light exists; it is the illusion of an absence of love. We can seek out light and love and lift our emotions to the higher vibration of light and love that is everywhere present.

Just as our thoughts are determined by our focus, it is our focus that determines the emotions that are present in any given moment. While there are many things in this world that seem to invite negative feelings, things that seemingly drag us in to the depths of despair, there is also an abundance of love. It is what we choose to see and ultimately feel that creates the emotions in our lives.

Nurturing ourselves emotionally is not denying the dark times we experience, it is finding the light as we move through the dark. Many great teachers have told us, we will never defeat the dark by adding more darkness, only light can do that. It is finding the love amid the experience and holding to that. There is no shame in feeling the dark emotions. We should never condemn ourselves for hurting or being angry or falling into the darkness. There is love and learning even there and often, the greatest learning comes while in that darkness and holding hope that all is well.

We nurture ourselves emotionally when we embrace our truth. We nurture ourselves emotionally when we embrace what resonates as goodness within. When we spend time acknowledging the light within that we can give to ourselves and our relationship, we elevate the emotional vibration that we feel and express.

Nurturing Our Spiritual Self
The spiritual self is that part of us that is wholly connected to God, Source, Higher Power. It is in this connection we find hope and faith. It is our spiritual selves that open awareness to the truth of who we are. It is here that we realize the limits we once believed about ourselves are merely illusions. It is our spiritual self that offers unconditional love to us and others we meet in our lives.

We nurture our spiritual selves through mindful awareness. With this awareness, we realize we are never alone, we are never without love and guidance. Tuning into our spiritual self allows us to more fully feel and express love and kindness in all we do.

It is in recognizing and embracing our spiritual truths that we empower our physical, mental and emotional selves to heal and radiate within us and out into the world. When we express from our spiritual selves, we radiate truth, love, peace, gratitude, compassion and understanding. When we radiate these, we not only heal and nurture ourselves, we heal and nurture our relationships and ultimately the world.

115

We create ripples of love and light that spread far beyond anything we can imagine.

The task of nurturing ourselves can seem daunting as we look at each individual part of us. When we take another look, though, we can recognize that nurturing one aspect of ourselves aids in nurturing another part of us. We will find that nurturing the physical aspect also creates an energy that promotes nurturing in the mental and emotional aspects. When we change our thoughts in the mental aspect, we change our attitudes about our physical needs and we enlighten our emotional self. When we truly embrace our spiritual truths and nurture this aspect of our being, we lift and nurture all others.

When we nurture ourselves on all levels and harmonize them all into our experience and expression of life, we turn our thoughts from "What am I looking for in this life?" to "What is the greatest gift I feel I bring to this life?" Instead of asking "Am I really getting what I need?" we ask, "Am I really giving all I have?" The truth is, all aspects of our being are already harmonized. We must simply open our awareness to each and nurture our whole self.

Here is a short list of ways we can nurture ourselves.

➢ Obviously, diet and exercise are wonderful places to begin. When our body is well, there are less limitations in our physical abilities and the mental fog of chaos and busyness clear. This clarity offers greater understanding of our truth. When we are physically well, our emotions lean towards the positive and our Spiritual self has less barriers to over-come.

➤ Checking in throughout the day to what thoughts are playing in our mind holds great benefits. Consider each thought and how it serves highest good. We can release those that limit us and embrace those that serve us.

➤ One of the best practices I have found to assist with nurturing is breath. A wonderful practice, I call The Three Breath Awareness, is an amazing resource to calm the mind. This is simply taking three mindful breaths. (Focus on your breath. Breathing in, know that you are breathing in. Breathing out, know that you are breathing out.) Along with silencing the mind chatter, this practice calms the physical body, as well. Our heart rate slows, our breathing becomes much deeper and provides an inflow of oxygen far greater than the shallow breathing we do throughout most of our day just to survive.

➤ Take walks. Any walk is beneficial to our blood flow and oxygen intake. Those who are confined to working in an office can benefit from regular breaks and walks around the building. Taking the stairs instead of using an elevator or escalator provides movement for the body. If the job or schedule prevents us from taking walks, we can practice stretching exercises at our desks. Wherever we spend our days, we can find ways to regularly integrate movement into our daily routine.

➤ Meditation is another beneficial resource to nurturing ourselves. We can meditate on our spiritual self, our truth, our goodness. We can meditate on loving ourselves and others more deeply and unconditionally. We can meditate on our connection to God. When we meditate, we calm our minds and free ourselves from limiting beliefs.

➢ At the beginning of each day, ask, "How can I more fully nurture me today?" Take time to listen for an answer and then put into motion that which you hear.

➢ At the end of each day, ask, "How did I nurture myself today?" Do not judge, criticize or compare your actions to your expectations, to other people or to what you have done before. Simply ask, receive an answer and be grateful for what comes. Even if the answer is "I did nothing to nurture myself," you have a place to begin tomorrow. And, know this, by simply asking the questions, you are nurturing you. So, no matter what, when you consider how to nurture you, you are giving attention to your well-being.

There is no template that we can study to find the best way to nurture ourselves as everyone is an individual and has individual requirements. Just as each of us are individuals, so are the methods we use to nurture and grow. We each have the opportunity to create our own template. We must remember though, the template that works today may need adjustment tomorrow. We serve ourselves best with our mindful awareness of what is working and what is not working in each moment. Leaving judgment out of the mix, tune in, be flexible. We are amazing creators and we can create or re-create our method of nurturing each moment of each day. When we are open to new ideas, new feelings, new awareness, we nurture ourselves no matter what else may be occurring in our lives.

Nurturing ourselves re-energizes us throughout our life experiences and it connects us with our authentic truth. Once we connect with our authenticity, we can live from that place. We often give up who we are in order to be the person we think we are supposed to be in any given situation. It is our choice and responsibility to stand in our truth, always. This is an invitation to allow the love we have for ourselves to stand strong in all situations. It is an invitation to allow our goodness and our love to rise above and beyond all that hinders us from experiencing the life we desire.

We can only give to our relationships that which we have within ourselves. Nurturing ourselves elevates and expands the love available to share into our relationships.

Forgive

One of the most empowering actions we can take to strengthen our relationship is to forgive. Forgiveness brings healing and love back into the mix, and in the process of forgiving, we transform the resentment, anger and other negative feelings that serve only to hinder love and peace. However, there are many beliefs about forgiveness that stand in our way.

Forgiveness is one of the most misunderstood statements and actions in our lives. Somewhere along the line we were taught we must forgive and forget. It is difficult, if not impossible, to forget. Now, this is not an excuse to continue harping on the things that brought us to resentment, anger and other negative feelings. It does mean that we release the hold these things have on us. Because of this, we often do not even consider forgiving as an option. Forgiving is not about forgetting.

In other circumstances, we define forgiving as "giving in." This feeling is contrary to our belief that we should stand our ground when we feel we are right. We often think that since the other person's actions are the cause of our resentments and anger, they should be the one to change and ask for forgiveness.

Forgiving from a place of ego feels like a loss. Ego tells us we will lose in the situation. It tells us we will lose our rightness. Ego convinces us we will be less valuable when we forgive, and it tells us that to forgive is to give permission to others to continue the behaviors that brought us the pain and anguish in the first place. Ego tells us that if we forgive, we are weak.

The truth is that holding on to our anger, resentment and the experience that caused it all does nothing but hurt us. It weakens us. Heart issues, stress, anxiety and other related illnesses are on the rise today and can be directly related to holding onto negative emotions. Our inability or unwillingness to forgive drives much of this and creates much more darkness and damage to our well-being, as well.

I was blessed with the experience of an incredible seminar more than twenty-five years ago. One of the exercises in the seminar was called the "Prison Visualization." This experience taught me the power of forgiveness, and the freedom the process brought has stayed with me to this day.

In this visualization, the participants were asked to think of someone we held resentment or anger towards. We were then guided to see them behind bars, in a jail cell, where we believed they belonged. Obviously, every jail must have a guard; guess who that guard is? We each are the guard of the jail cell we created. We are the judge, jury, guard, warden and maybe even the executioner. That may sound cruel but anytime we hold resentment or anger towards someone, we have put them on trial, judged and sentenced them and believe we are holding them prisoner.

We were then instructed to vividly see our prisoner in that jail cell. We pictured their face, their demeanor, their actions. It was not long until we all had a very clear picture of the person and the actions that caused them to be imprisoned in our minds. We then saw a very clear picture of the solitary guard standing vigil night and day over the jail - ourselves. Each of us was standing guard in the hall just outside the steel bars of the cell we created so that the prisoners could not leave.

121

Our teacher then asked us to look a little more closely at the jail cell. The cell door was not keeping the others imprisoned, it had imprisoned us. The people we thought we had imprisoned were actually living their lives; they were still playing with friends and family, going about their business and carrying on with life. We had created the illusion that we had them under lock and key, however, they were not the ones being burdened with pain and suffering; we were. We were still guarding the locked door. The question was asked, "So who truly is the prisoner?"

While we stand guard, we are not free. As long as we believe the illusion that we are holding others in a prison, so they suffer and pay for their actions or words, we are not free.

Forgiveness is not about saying what was done to us was right, good or okay. It is about saying we are not going to let it hold us back from living our own life. Forgiveness is not about telling the other person we are going to open ourselves up for them to do it again. It is about saying, I am strong enough to overcome this and I now have choices to make in my own life and I will not be hurt like that again.

There will be things in this life and our relationships that will hurt. We are going to experience darkness and negativity. When we allow those experiences to limit our experience of life, we are volunteering to be a victim. Anytime we allow an experience or person to have power over us, we forfeit our power and volunteer to be a victim.

In relationships, it is easy to feel as if our partner has the power to make us feel one way or the other. Believing this is to surrender our own authority over our thoughts and feelings. When we practice authentic forgiveness, we become our own hero; we claim our power and we rise above the pain and suffering. Forgiveness is seeing the light and truth that lie beyond the hurtful experience. It is seeing the authenticity of our partner more than the error that was made. Forgiveness empowers us to freely and authentically live again.

Forgiving our partner is essential to the relationship. Without forgiveness, darkness piles upon darkness and soon it is difficult to imagine a way back to the relationship we once hoped and worked for. In forgiving, we enable ourselves to see the partner we have loved. We regain hope and we look forward to what comes next.

As huge as forgiving our partner is, there is one more person we must forgive, and we must do it often. We must forgive ourselves. We must forgive ourselves of our part in every circumstance we live that does not serve our highest good. Whether we contributed to the initial action or not, we carry the weight of how we feel in and from that action. If, in our pain, we withheld love, we contributed to the negativity and darkness of the action. If we blamed, judged or compared our partners, we withheld love. For that, we must forgive ourselves.

We are also, very often, our own worst critics. We are often mean, cruel and hurtful to ourselves. What do we say to ourselves when we look in the mirror and see those extra five pounds? What do we say to ourselves when we make a mistake at something we should have managed perfectly; or even things we are trying for the first time? What do we think of ourselves when we say hurtful things to our spouse in reaction to an unpleasant situation?

It is easy to be rough on ourselves. We say things to ourselves that we would not dream of saying to someone else. We abuse ourselves by neglecting to nurture our well-being. We neglect our true feelings and desires by looking outside of ourselves for ways to validate our own worth.

Forgiving self is essential. When we offer ourselves kindness, we create a foundation from which more kindness can grow. Love and peace and understanding grow as well. Judging only leads to more judging, sentencing and guarding. Creating harmony and love within, allows us to more fully express harmony and love to others.

We can truly forgive all we have done to ourselves. When we do, we open that jail cell door and can more easily forgive others for what we perceive they have done. We can relinquish the guard duty and soar into our own lives. When we forgive self and others, we can live as we are meant to live; a free spirit rising ever higher and higher. As we rise, we elevate our partner and our relationship.

A beautiful tool taught in the seminar I mentioned, is the Anger To Love Letter. This letter assists us in transforming the feelings of pain we perceive were caused by people, things, situations or self. It is an actual letter and it can be given to the person we feel hurt us or it can be kept to ourselves. The giving of the letter may feel necessary in some cases; however, the power of this letter is in writing and feeling it.

The letter begins; Dear (person, situation, etc.) When _____ happened, I felt _____.

From here, we express the pain and anger and sorrow; any negative feelings that arose from the instance. We express these feelings until we cannot express them any further. Write without censoring. Just allow the words and feelings to flow from within onto the page.

Once we have fully expressed the negative feelings and thoughts onto the page, we then transition to a more positive outlook and express what we learned about ourselves or the other person from the situation. If negativity or anger creep back in, we return to the anger portion of the letter, express those feelings and thoughts and continue. It is important that we do not speed through this first segment of expressing ourselves; there is no time limit. Once we have fully expressed our negative emotions, we can turn more fully to awareness of growth and learning that are available.

When we have written the lessons and awareness we found, we open awareness to the love we have for the person or situation or self. We literally write everything we love about our partner or self. We express only love and light and peace.

When we have written all we feel is needed, we forgive. Remember, forgiving is releasing the other person from the responsibility of our feelings, it is releasing ourselves from the darkness we carried. When we forgive, we also forgive ourselves of our part in the situation. Even if our part was only carrying the pain for a while, we forgive ourselves.

In this exercise, we write from our hearts. We do not worry about grammar or spelling or "right" words. We simply write our feelings until we have expressed all that needs be expressed. Once we have transformed the darkness into freedom, we can then decide to share the letter or keep it. We can save it or destroy it. The power of this process is in the experience of transformation offered in the release of emotions that hinder us from fully opening to authentic living.

Forgiveness is necessary in all relationships. Even if the error seems slight, it deserves our forgiveness. Forgive situations, forgive words, forgive partners, forgive self. Through forgiveness, we open that cell door that has kept us prisoner for far too long. In opening that door, we can fly, we can soar, we can be the authentic self we are designed to be.

In forgiving, we create an atmosphere where love can grow. Whether we are forgiving ourselves, our partners or situations, we release the darkness and move into the light. When we let go of blame and anger, we clean the slate in our minds where only limitations existed before and we create thoughts of possibilities. Through forgiveness, we open our hearts to create new pathways to authentic love.

Fully Value Your Relationship

Just how much value do you place on your relationship? How much do you place on your partner? And how about you? Many people answer with a resounding "Very Much."

Before we move on, define "Very Much." I am not asking for a dictionary definition, just be clear on what it means to you.

That which we value the most is that which we spend the most energy and time on. The more we value something, the more we focus on it. Now this is not to say that we love the thing we spend the most time on more than our relationship. Love and value here are not the same thing. To value something, we honor it through our attention. We take steps to insure it is cared for and protected.

Relationships tend to be taken for granted. How much time and energy are spent on caring for and keeping safe the relationship? How much effort is put into growing the relationship? How much time is actually spent tuning into the happiness, sadness, frustration, bliss, or any other feelings in the relationship?

The value we put on something is equal to the importance we put on it. Value is not determined by how important it is supposed to be. That standard is put in place by the environment around each person. Our parents will play a big part in this as will our religious beliefs, media, friends, television shows and on and on. The truth is that the value we place on any given thing is really about the importance we give to that thing. Just because we think something is supposed to be a high value item does not mean it holds that value in our lives. Becoming aware of where we place our relationship in the value hierarchy is important to our peace and happiness as well as the success of our relationship.

The fact that we love our partner and care about the status of the relationship does not translate into valuing it. It is possible to care about something deeply but have no desire to devote time and energy to building it up. Unfortunately, many people jump into relationships because it is something they believe they "should" do.

We may very well love our partner but have no energy to build the relationship. We may be perfectly happy with where the relationship stands and as long as our partner is in agreement, and we have open communications about it, there may be no apparent problems. These relationships just coast along, never gaining momentum.

Now, most people prefer to elevate and expand their relationship and to do that, we must fully value the relationship, our partner and ourselves. To know where our relationship and our partner stand in the hierarchy of values in our life, we must simply look at how much time we spend devoted to them.

Upon learning this fact about time equaling value, many people argue the point. One of the most common arguments is that they must work so much to pay the bills that they are unable to spend time within the relationship. Obviously, work is a high valued part of life for most people. If you spend more time focused on work than you do your relationship, work has a higher value.

Notice, I use the word *focused* here. We can be at work for ten hours a day and when our focus is on lovingly providing for our family, then our relationship and family holds a high value. If, on the other hand, we spend our time at home focused on work instead of family, our job is valued higher than our relationship. Be cautious though, sometimes the work we do is more about getting that new car or home or nicer clothes or a country club membership, and it is all done under the illusion that these things will enhance the relationship. Material things will never enrich a relationship; only love and attention can do that. Those material items may be nice to have and there is no condemnation here for wanting these things; we must simply understand what holds the greatest value.

We can become vigilant in raising the value of our relationship through intention. When our intention is set on elevating and expanding our relationship, all we do can elevate the relationship. With intentions set towards enriching the relationship, working ten hours or more each day will not prevent us from lifting our relationship.

Our intentions are a beautiful and perfect guide as they will alert us to when things are veering off course. Beginning the day with a daily practice of reviewing intentions will keep the most valued things in focus, even when our days become chaotic. Our intention will direct our attention to what truly matters in life and all will be well.

To create an increasingly higher level of value on the relationship, we can shift the relationship more and more into our focus through our intentions. It does not mean we have to physically be standing next to our partner each moment of the day. This simply means that we can keep the relationship in our focus when we are dealing with other obligations, and we can look for ways to enrich the time we are physically with our partner.

When we honestly consider where our relationships, partners and selves are on the value scale, we can take conscious action to lift them up. When we are blind to this, we may feel that we are elevating our relationship, when in reality, we are taking it for granted. Valuing the relationship is not about adding more to-dos to our already full schedules; it is about adding value to the things we already do, the time we are able to spend together, and the attention and intention we give.

Expanding, adding and creating value in our relationships enrich far more than the relationship. The added value enriches our lives inside and outside of the relationship. By consciously adding value, we shift our intention to higher levels of love and this additional love radiates within, to our partners and to the world.

Embrace Uniqueness

Each person on this planet has their own unique personalities, and they all culminate into the experience offered in this life journey. The uniqueness we each have to offer includes our specific traits, strengths, behaviors, beliefs and opinions, as well as the unique fears, weaknesses, feelings, etc. There are no two people who are identical. Even those of you who may be an identical twin are unique. Each person walking upon this planet and all those who came before us and all who are yet to come are unique, different, individual.

We can all be grateful for the uniqueness of the individuals in this world, even the fears and perceived weaknesses, as this life experience would be a very dull place without those differences.

As beautiful as these differences can be, there are many people who see the differences as a threat to their own security and worth. Some people are fine with differences as long as those who are different are completely segregated from their lifestyle. There are those who think that anyone different from them is less than or lacking. Differences are seen by some as an attack on their own way of life. Some people see these differences as indicators of worth. If you hold similarities to one group, you may be seen as worthy of being with them while traits you have that are different from the group could cast away all of your worth in their eyes.

Racism is still a very visible example of what happens when we choose to see through the eyes of ignorance and cluster people of the same color, religion, ethnicity, nationality, or any other label, into one category and define them as all the same. In doing this, generalized definitions are placed on the people of that group and the individuals lose their identity in the eyes of the person doing the categorizing.

We do this in our relationships as well. It is a common behavior to grasp the commonalities we have with our partner and attempt to remove the differences. Instead of embracing the differences as an opportunity to expand our own experience of life, we attempt to mold our partner into what we define as the perfect partner or an exact replica of ourselves.

When we allow these limiting beliefs about differences to dictate our belief about a person or group, we are practicing and promoting judgment, and even racism to some degree. And folks, all levels of judgment and racism or any other kind of negative belief about others cause pain and suffering for the other person or group and ourselves.

When we do not embrace differences, we are guilty of judgment and comparison, which we covered earlier in this book. This judgment and comparison cheat us out of seeing the possibilities available to us and we cheat the other person from expressing as their own authentic self. Seeing the differences as bad, wrong or less than lead us to this type of thinking, and this thinking is truly based on ignorance, not truth.

(Just so we are clear, ignorance is defined as lack of knowledge, education and/or awareness.)

When we base our perception of others and self on anything less than understanding and awareness, we do not see the entirety of that which we are perceiving. Again, we cheat ourselves and harm others.

The dynamics between us and those close to us, our partner, close friends and family, are no different than what we see on the global scale. Our personal relationships are merely a mirror of how we view the world and vice versa. To see differences as opportunities and resources, we must remind ourselves that each person is an individual, unique and different from us. Because of this beautiful and wonderful fact, each person deserves to be seen as the authentic individual that they are designed to be. To wish for anything else is like wishing for a Ferrari to behave like a Smart Car because our definition of our perfect car says that is the way it should be. It is like wishing your cabin cruiser was like your john boat because that is what you have experienced all your life.

We sometimes lump our partners into certain categories defined by our comparisons to others and then treat them in the same way we treat every other person in that category. Simply because our partner may enjoy heavy metal rock instead of the country music we may enjoy, does not make them a heavy partier and unreliable in the faithful department. Simply because our partner may choose to wear their ball cap backwards does not automatically make them a gangster out looking for trouble. Skin color, fashion preferences, beliefs, fears and every other unique trait of our partners and ourselves is what make us individuals and that individuality is to be celebrated and honored

We all bring past experiences into the relationship, as well. No matter how much we may have worked to leave it all behind and attempted to begin anew, our perceptions, beliefs and feelings are affected by things we lived through since the day we were born and the same holds true for our partners. We all carry our own unique baggage. The beauty of this life experience is that each one of us is unique. Even though there are more than seven billion other people breathing air on this earth right now, we are all unique. The only thing not unique about us is that we are all unique.

So, to practice embracing uniqueness, we must first look at how we are unique individuals. We must identify our unique traits and qualities; not to set us apart from our partners but to open awareness to what we have to offer the relationship. Once we understand the uniqueness we bring to the relationship, we can look at the unique traits of our partners and see what they bring.

Even though our uniqueness is a beautiful expression which we can share with others and ourselves, even though these unique traits within us create a beautiful experience of life, many of us still tend to shy away from allowing our uniqueness to shine, or we attempt to stifle the uniqueness of our partners.

One of the reasons we hide our own uniqueness is that to let it shine, we must become vulnerable. In allowing our own light to shine, we must allow those pieces of us that make us unique from others an opportunity to be seen. To allow our truest self to radiate from us, we must show that unique part of us to others and that truth very well may be judged by others. We must reveal that part of ourselves that is unlike any other person. Each time we allow our uniqueness to be seen, the ego driven thoughts chime in telling us we are not good enough and we may not be liked or loved anymore.

Vulnerability really does feel scary and weak, but it does not have to be. Vulnerability really can become an empowering motivator. It can be a strength that propels us through life situations, it can be a beautiful reminder that we are unique, and it can be an invitation to let our uniqueness shine. When we embrace vulnerability with this attitude and understanding, we gift ourselves, our partners and others the truth that is within us.

To be ourselves means we are choosing to not copy anyone else just to fit in and that often opens us to ridicule from others. We almost need to take on an attitude of "I don't care what others think." I am not suggesting that we actually adopt this attitude as we are naturally compassionate people and compassion prevents us from not caring. Instead of not caring, we can simply think to ourselves or even say out loud, "My amazing unique self deserves to shine and as I shine; I honor the unique in you."

Remember that in living uniquely, we are choosing to not let the other person's opinions outweigh our own. We are allowing our truth to resonate with the truth of others. In expressing as our unique selves, we are creating opportunities to experience unique and unlimited relationships. And as we gift ourselves with the opportunities found by being unique, we can gift our partners the same opportunities.

I want to share with you a statement made to me many years ago by one of my coaches that has been extremely empowering in my walk to uniqueness. I was told, "What others think about me is none of my business." While this was difficult to swallow, it has opened many miles of positive progress on my life journey.

Aside from being vulnerable, another reason we shy away from showing our unique traits is that we have simply been taught to conform. We have essentially been brain-washed throughout our lives to think we should not be different; we have been told that we should just blend in.

Conformity and blending cause us to fall into the "should" frame of mind. My dear friend, Pam Aks, teaches that we all too often fall into the behavior she calls, "shoulding all over ourselves." We get stuck believing that we should do this, and we should do that when really, we should do nothing. Carrying around all the "shoulds" only serves to add to the burdens and stress in our day. "Shoulding" all over ourselves keeps us in a constant state of catching up. We never have time to relax and just be our unique selves when we are constantly telling ourselves we should be something else.

We have choices and there is no "should." Yes, there are consequences to our choices. However, we get to decide what choice we want to make. We can decide if those consequences are acceptable or if we will even accept them at all. We are unique.

As if "shoulding" on ourselves was not enough, our ego steps in and creates many more illusions. Ego tries to sell us on the belief that we are better off conforming. Ego then takes that belief and adds reasons why we should never step out of line. It tells us things like we are less than, we are not good enough, we do not deserve to be unique and therefore we should remain lemmings following the crowd towards the cliff. Listen to the ego only long enough to know when it is directing you away from something wonderful. That is a good sign there is something worth looking at right in front of you.

Uniqueness suffers a mighty blow as television, internet, magazine and radio ads constantly tell us we need to conform. We need to be like everybody else; we need to buy certain items, so we can be cool and fit in. We are told we must live in the right part of town if we want to fit in. We are told we must behave a certain way if we want to get ahead in the world.

These ads even tell us that if we want to be unique we must have certain haircuts or phones or clothes; you get the picture. Consider this, if we believe the ads and accept that the item or look is what makes us cool, then, are we not giving up our uniqueness? After all, the ads are telling everyone who watches the same thing. If we all bought into the pitch, we would all look the same and ultimately act the same. When we buy the item that is supposed to make us unique, we are buying the same item that thousands if not millions of others have bought as well. How unique is that?

Fortunately, the items we buy and the looks we desire have little to do with our unique contribution to this life or our relationships. Our uniqueness is found within; not out in the world somewhere. To find the answers we seek, we must mindfully connect with our essence, our heart our higher power, God, The Universe, our Source. The answers outside of us are not answers at all but merely illusions.

Having considered these ways that cause us to limit our own unique, we must also be aware that our partners are experiencing the same things. They too find themselves vulnerable. They too tend to conform. They too "should on themselves," and they too see the multitude of ads telling them they must be a certain way.

We can embrace our own unique and support our partners in embracing their unique. When we allow our unique attribute to shine and encourage our partners to do the same, we strengthen the foundation of our relationship and that can propel our partnership into levels never before attained.

The benefits of expressing as your unique self and allowing your partner to do the same are incredible. Uniqueness is what brings about positive change, new ideas, new opportunities and much more. We have all benefited greatly from those who chose to embrace their uniqueness. Just think of where we would be if everyone throughout history chose to hide their uniqueness. What would life be like if everyone chose to think like everyone else?

For one, there would be no original thought. No one would have chosen to use fire for warmth or cooking and certainly not for ambiance. There certainly would be no wheel so no vehicles would be around to carry us from point A to point B. We would all still believe the earth to be flat. There would never have been any great spiritual leaders, no teachers, no innovators; no forward thinking at all. Technology would be non-existent. Every person would be exactly the same; the way we look, the way we act, what we believe, the things we like and dislike.

When we all decide to hide our unique traits and qualities, life becomes very dull. Some people believe acting on our uniqueness is a form of self-promoting bravado or showing off, so they hide their unique. Some religions teach that being unique is a sin we need to steer clear of, which, to me, is absolutely hilarious since all religions are built upon the teachings or the lives of extremely unique teachers. The truth is, we are born as unique individuals and any attempt to hold ourselves back from that truth is in conflict to our very nature. We are designed to be unique, not necessarily to stand out and perceive that we are better than others but to offer our uniqueness to the world as a beacon to truth.

In fact, to see the truth of this statement we need only look at nature. In nature there is uniqueness in every living creature, every tree, every rock, every grain of sand, every wave - everything. This uniqueness in nature is the very thing that makes this world such a beautiful place. If everything in existence is unique, is it so hard to believe we are uniquely built as well? We are part of nature, so would it be such a leap to accept that we too are made as unique individuals?

138

By accepting our unique qualities and traits as our truth and by allowing them to flow from us, we create a more fulfilling life for ourselves, our partners and others around us. When we embrace our unique, we are no longer in resistance to our truth. We will live a happier life. We will feel more peaceful and confident in our daily living and our relationships will blossom.

In expressing our uniqueness in our relationships, we share new thoughts and new ideas. We explore different ways of seeing things and empower ourselves to discover even more of our own truths and the truths of our partners. We open ourselves to imagine bigger and we allow our partners imagination a chance to expand as well. Imagining bigger allows us to believe bigger. In this, hope grows into faith and our courage to explore the perceived limits of our personal and relationship comfort zones expand and elevate.

In this expanded perception of ourselves, our whole attitude positively shifts, our self-awareness expands, and we can see the good of our uniqueness. We more fully understand that our partner and everyone else are also unique. They too have their own ideas, thoughts, actions and so on. They are individual and deserve, just as we do, to be unique. When we can see this in our partners, we have truly grown to a point where judgments no longer serve us. We can understand that difference does not translate as negative but does promote positive discovery. We can see the truth that our partner's unique trait does not create lack or wrong in ourselves. Our partner's unique need not warrant fear in us.

Using our unique traits and qualities creates a snowball effect for good. As we create new thoughts and actions from our uniqueness, our relationship and our world grow. We see more of the world around us. We live more

139

deeply in all we do. We experience more of what life has to offer.

Unique does not mean coming up with something entirely new in every waking moment. It does not mean to change you just to be different. It is simply doing everything you do as the unique individual you are and in your own unique and individual way.

While we need not change just to be unique, we are already that, we must be willing to be flexible in what our uniqueness is for us and allow our partners to be flexible in their unique. The entirety of the Universe is continuously expanding and elevating. We and our partners are also continuously expanding and elevating. With each unique experience we have, our uniqueness grows. When we allow our uniqueness to breathe, we see things differently, we judge less, we are more accepting and understanding, and we open ourselves to love more, which leads to more free use of our unique traits and qualities, which leads to greater trust in our uniqueness, which leads to more trust and willingness to allow our uniqueness to live. As this continues, we create an ever-enlightening cycle to be realized as opposed to the vicious cycle we often fall into as we hide our truth.

We have been encouraged all along the journey of our life to buy into the belief that it was better to blend in than stand out. Most of us have tried being a carbon copy of someone else and most of us have worked diligently at creating the relationship that someone else portrayed as perfect. Remember this: it takes more energy to deny our truth and convert ourselves into an exact replica of someone else than it does to simply flow with what comes from our heart. This is true whether we are considering our personal

140

life journey or our relationship. Allowing our relationship to be unique is a gift and a blessing we can embrace.

We have heard all our lives that we are all created equal. That is true. We are equally unique. Because of this truth, we realize we are not above anyone else, and we are not below anyone either.

Be your own brand of unique and embrace it. Let the authentic you shine, allow your partner's authentic self to shine and together be a source of light to the world.

Practice Authentic Communications

Authentic communication is comprised of four practices. While they are presented here as four separate tools, the added value and enriched communication methods come when they are all practiced together. For the sake of learning them, take one at a time and try it on. See how it fits, how it resonates within you. Once comfortable with one, bring in the next and continue until you have all four working together. Even though these four practices combine to create a powerful communication tool, they do stand alone and can be used individually as the need arises.

Listen with The Intent to Understand

Listening with the intent to understand is one of the greatest communication tools we can practice in our relationships and our lives. Until we understand, we stand little or no chance to work through the issues in our relationships and life. When we understand our partner, we have little need for "making stuff up" about their actions and words; judgments and comparisons are no longer needed. When we fully understand ourselves, we communicate our thoughts more clearly and lovingly leaving little room for misinterpretation.

Most people do not listen with the intent to understand; they listen with the intent to reply. The cause of many arguments and disagreements we face in the world today, as well as our relationships, rise from this truth. Effective communication tools are not usually used as part of our conversations and in some cases, they are being intentionally ignored. In many conversations, listening does not even come into the mix. Talking over people, bullying others into submission to ideas and complete disregard for others' thoughts and opinions dictate much of what is considered communication these days.

The sad thing about this is that we are giving up one of the greatest tools possible for growth and expansion of our knowledge and experience of life and relationships when we refuse to listen to others. Listening with the intent to understand does not mean we must forget what we think or believe; it does not mean we must surrender our beliefs or thoughts to others. "Listening with The Intent to Understand" means that hearing what is actually being said opens the door to an amazing understanding and can even lead to a new way of perceiving or experiencing something. In using this tool, we do not abandon our own beliefs, thoughts and ideas; however, we may greatly expand upon them when we authentically listen. When we do not effectively listen, we miss this beautiful gift.

When communications fail, things begin to snowball from there. A misunderstanding can lead to loss of trust, anger, sadness, a sense of loneliness and more. It is not until we shift our way of communicating that we can prevent the avalanche of issues heading our way. No matter how much we love someone, no matter how much we desire happiness and goodness in our relationships, intimate and otherwise, we will never know true peace, love and happiness until we find understanding.

The understanding we seek is far beyond the words that are spoken. Listening with the intent to understand opens us to the feelings and intentions the other person is expressing.

In relationships, no matter what reasons couples claim when they file for divorce, communication breakdowns cause nearly every breakup. Conversely, if communication skills are used, greater understanding of our partner's communication can lead to resolution and growth. Most problems at work can be resolved with empowered communication. Many of the global problems can be solved if only the powers that govern would be open to have authentic communications.

While social media and the awesome technologies of today have made it easier to stay connected to others, they have also become a source that further damages authentic communications. With the advancement of technology, we are losing the personal touch; we are losing our authentic connections.

This is not to say that authentic connections are not possible through social media. I have developed several wonderful relationships on-line. After seven years of on-line friendship, I finally met a dear friend in person and the connection was as authentic as if we were neighbors for that whole time.

The use of social media makes it easier for us to allow our communications skills to take a break.

It is up to each of us to make changes and enhance our communication skills if we want to truly connect with others and ultimately lead our lives and even the world to peace and well-being.

The thing to remember here is that communication errors are not always obvious or blatant failures. We often do not even realize we have made a communication error until the energy of the conversation or relationship shifts. In our fast-paced lifestyles we have begun to hurry through everything we do, and our conversations and communications are not excluded. Even with our partners, we rush communication, so we can get on to the next project. In this need for speed, we have learned many shortcuts which amount to ways not to communicate throughout our lives.

When we are receiving information from someone, whether it be a work-related, a domestic issue or a romantic conversation, hearing the actual words spoken and listening beyond those words open us to understanding. When we become vested enough to seek understanding, we validate the speaker with our attention and we validate ourselves with understanding. With understanding we can respond appropriately. When others feel heard, the relationship elevates and expands.

Communicate with Flexibility

Authentic communications do not stop with hearing and understanding others. We must also be authentic in the message we send out and the way we send it. When we are speaking, we serve communications, the relationship, our partner and ourselves greatly with the use of the tool, "Communicate with Flexibility". Again, the fast-paced lifestyle most of us have adopted brings us to the belief that we have no time for authentic communication.

We tend to race through our conversations, we abbreviate our conversations, we use letters instead of complete words in our texts and emails, we even use emojis in place of a written or verbal response. As a society, we have adopted a "faster is better" mentality, and we look for as many shortcuts as we can find.

Shortcuts are not reserved for communications either. We use them everywhere in our lives, including our health and wellness. Shortcuts cheat us of being fully present and mindful and we miss much of life. Using shortcuts while delivering our message cheat us of fully expressing what we want to say, and it cheats our partners of hearing our heart. When we use these shortcuts, we are giving permission to the one we are communicating with to make up their own story about our message.

To Communicate with Flexibility, we must be fully present in our communications, and we must be complete in our conversations. The shortcuts de-value what it is we are saying. We must be mindful of our experience within the conversation. When we are fully present while communicating with our partners, we expand love and understanding. Our message is heard and understood on a much deeper level. The time we take to ensure complete understanding on our part and the part of others is more than redeemed due to the unified energetic flow towards the intent of the conversation.

Communicating with flexibility also includes being flexible in how we speak our messages. One of the communication errors I frequently witness is when someone makes a statement and the other person does not understand or know the answer. Most of the time the first person says the same exact thing over again, only louder.

A couple near me at a restaurant fell into this trap. The woman made a comment to which her husband replied, "What?" She repeated her words exactly as she had spoken them originally, only louder. He again asked, "What?" This happened seven times and each time the words were the same and the volume went up. It was obvious to those of us sitting close by that this was not a matter of failed hearing but one of not understanding.

Getting louder will not make the point any clearer. If the tool, "Listening with the Intent to Understand" would have been used by the person receiving the statement, he could have asked for clarity and the sender could have explained differently or more deeply. If the sender of information knew the "Communicate with Flexibility" tool, she would have expanded the way she spoke her information at the first sign of misunderstanding. There are many things that could have been done to come to understanding.

Communicating with flexibility expands clarity and creates an atmosphere where understanding is possible. Be flexible enough to restate in different words and phrases so that the recipient can understand. It is not completely the receiver's responsibility to get your point, it is primarily yours. Having said that, if you are the one who does not understand, instead of saying "huh" or "what" over and over, be brave enough to admit that you do not understand. It does not make us stupid if the message sent is given in such a way as to not make since to us; ask for clarity.

It is not that we do not see eye to eye as much as we are not communicating flexibly enough to fully express our needs or understand the point of view of others. Miscommunication prevents us from working towards

147

agreements and resolutions. Until we become flexible in our communications and truly hear what is being said, we can never really find solutions. When we do listen and hear and when we do speak from a place of authenticity with a desire for understanding, we can find results in every situation that work for all involved.

Do You Mean?

I was introduced to a communication game that has become a staple in my communication toolbox and is invaluable in my relationship, work and everyday life. It is called "Do You Mean?" and it is far more than a game.

When we listen to someone tell us a story or send a message about anything at all, we can practice the "Do You Mean" tool. When they have concluded their story, we ask, "Do you mean?" and repeat back in our own words what we just heard. In doing this, several beautiful benefits occur. First, the person talking to us feels validated and heard. Next, we are communicating that we truly do want to understand their story. And, the other person has the opportunity to clarify anything we may have misinterpreted or missed.

When we are giving information or telling a story, we can reverse this tool and ask the other person to repeat back what they just heard. The benefits here are just as profound. They are once again validated because we are taking time to make sure they have all they need to understand the message and we are able to insure our message has been received.

The added benefit to both scenarios is that a foundation is built upon which resolution to problems, expanded experience and much more positive movement and growth can come. In using this tool, there is very little room for error whether the other person knows how to play the "Do You Mean Game" or not. Understanding is found, and flexibility is encouraged.

There are times we feel that we are doing a great job of communicating only to discover no understanding was achieved. Along with the previously mentioned causes of communication issues, many of our miscommunication arise from the words we use; or more accurately, the numerous definitions of the words we use. For example, define this statement, "They were tight."

I hear answers like:

They were close friends.
The nuts and bolts were put together firmly.
They were drunk.
They were stingy with their money.
They were in sync.
They worked well together.

The words we use are often not that reliable which is another great reason to use the tools presented here.

On top of all these communication hurdles, the way we process what people are saying to us leaves much room for miscommunication as well. Did you know that the words we use in our conversations only make up 7% of effective communication? Tone of voice comes in at 38% and body language makes up the remaining 55%. Imagine what this does to our communication reliability with all the texting and emails we rely on so heavily these days.

An unfortunate example of how failure to fully communicate can create havoc in our lives comes from a client who was based in one location while the staff he was leading was in another part of the country. The client and his staff were having discussions about the launch of a huge new project. All communications were done via phone due to an overfull schedule that did not allow face-to-face meetings. Daily phone calls led everyone to believe all was on track and heading in the right direction.

Three months into the project, the client was finally able to visit the other location to check on the progress. What he found was a disaster. His staff was totally off track from his intentions; three months had been wasted and huge amounts of money spent on something that was not part of the initial plan.

When we went back and looked at the communications between the offices, we found that the instructions were carried out perfectly; however, the instructions could be interpreted in more than one way. The staff had a completely different idea of the client's vision and had worked diligently towards those results.

When we assume our communications have been heard and understood and we fail to follow-up with flexible communications, the outcomes may be far different than the ideas in our mind. We may assume that all is well while our partners have a totally different assumption as to the meaning of our message.

These assumptions, on the relationship level, lead to communication breakdowns which in turn create unnecessary stress on the relationship and can become relationship breakdowns on many levels. Failure to fully communicate is a primary cause of romantic break-ups, family tensions, loss of friends, and the loss of peace in our lives. On a global scale, communication breakdowns can easily lead to failed policies, tension between countries and even war.

I have heard from more than one person that it is not their responsibility when someone misinterprets what they say. Wrong! We are solely responsible for our message getting across correctly. If we do not care enough about what we have to say to make sure our intent is delivered, then maybe our statement does not need to be delivered in the first place.

Now if we take great measures to deliver the message in a way that the impact can equal our intent and it is still misunderstood, we have choices. We can continue looking for flexible ways to communicate the message or we can let the person know we are not on the same page and we can open a different dialogue about how to sync up. Of course, there are times complete understanding is achieved and the other person just does not agree with us, totally different topic.

Listen with the Intent to Understand, Communicate with Flexibility and practice Do You Mean; these will set us up to have meaningful communications with our partner, family, friends and everyone else we encounter. Communication is key to elevating and expanding relationships and all of life.

When we practice these three tools, communication mishaps are much less frequent, and we will enjoy greater understanding. As powerful as these tools can be in our lives, we can still run into miscommunication issues. With the use of this next tool, the backlash of miscommunication can be overcome. We will now move to the absolute greatest communication tool available for our toolbox.

Communicate with L.O.V.E.

This tool has tremendous and positive impact with everyone we meet, and it is essential to elevate and expand our most intimate relationship. Even when complete understanding is illusive, even when we cannot come to agreement or see eye to eye, this tool will allow us to remain loving and empathic in the conversation. The tool is "Communicate with L.O.V.E." This is a technique called the L.O.V.E. model which reminds us to Listen Openly; Validate Equally.

After more than 20 years of communication studies, through the work of many teachers, programs and books, I have learned 18 ways not to communicate effectively. Even though those studies revealed many ways not to communicate, only 1 way has been found that offers effective communications every time; the L.O.V.E. model. This statement does not negate the value of the tools discussed earlier in this chapter, they too are powerful. Each of the tools we have already discussed and many more play a part in getting us to the point where we can effectively communicate. When we practice the L.O.V.E model of communications, we find that authentic communications can still occur even if we forget to practice the others.

With the L.O.V.E. model, even if we do not understand the content of the conversation, we will find understanding of the other person's feelings. We find a deeper connection to them and open opportunity for a foundation to be built from which we can further our connection.

As mentioned, there are 18 common listening mistakes which include communication behaviors such as

Rehearsing, Bullying, Counter-attacking, Being Right, Dreaming, Evaluating/Judging, Giving Advice and Being Philosophical.

Each time we practice one of these, we devalue the content of the conversation, the other person and ourselves. We prevent the complete meaning and understanding of the conversation from being discovered. While some of these are practiced with good intentions, they only serve to move us further from a place of understanding and resolution. The L.O.V.E. Model replaces these non-working methods of communication.

The first part of the L.O.V. E. model is Listen Openly. This simply means to listen. We often burden ourselves with the belief that we should be able to "fix" whatever problem is being presented. We stress over ways to improve upon that which is said to us. We even fall into chaotic thinking sometimes when we feel that we need to have a response ready to go when the other person has completed their statement.

True understanding comes when we let go of the burdens and stress of responding or fixing and simply listen. More times than not, the needed solution or response presents itself when we listen openly. Even if the conversation does not require a solution and is simply a story telling moment, being free to hear without the need to respond in specific ways creates an atmosphere of trust and understanding.

Clearing our minds and simply hearing what our partner is saying allows us to share the moment. We can experience the story with them and nothing leads to understanding greater than shared experience. Clearing our minds of the chaotic response mechanism, we can hear beyond words and tune into the feelings and meanings our partners may not be able to put into words.

As we listen, we can release the stress of adding our interpretation to what is being said. We serve no one; not ourselves, our partners and certainly not the relationship by interpreting the content of the conversation differently than the one who spoke it.

It is our interpretation that often leads to miscommunication, argument and negativity. When we add our own interpretation or judgement, we send the message that our partners' words were not important enough to stand on their own. In listening openly, we send the message that we are here to support them, and we care enough to understand.

The next part of the L.O.V.E. model is Validate Equally. The "Do You Mean?" tool we learned earlier can be a wonderful asset here. We can state what we just heard without added interpretation or judgment and ask for clarification on the things we may have missed.

When we validate equally we show support, we acknowledge our partner's worthiness and we express love. To validate equally shows that we do not deem our partner's understanding of what they just shared as less important than or our interpretations.

Listen Openly; Validate Equally elevates understanding and from there, communications and relationships grow lovingly and powerfully. With understanding, we truly empower the partnership between ourselves and our partner.

Fix Nothing - Transform Everything

Our true nature is to love and along with this comes compassion. We are compassionate people which leads us to care about other's well-being. Along the journey of this life experience, we have learned that we must "fix" everything we perceive as broken or out of sync with our definition of what is right in life, relationships and our world. Our compassion for others leads us to repair what we perceive as wrong or broken; however, more times than not, the best thing we can do is offer support and leave the "fixing" to the person dealing with the situation.

The belief that we must fix all that is wrong or broken creates an unnecessary stress in our lives. We have opened ourselves to judge more deeply, to see things as right or wrong; good or bad. When we see things from this frame of mind, and heart, we fail to see the beautiful colors and textures of this life; we are stuck in black and white thinking.

Society's addiction to media, whether that be traditional network news or social media, keeps chaotic current events in front of us nearly all day, every day. We watch with good intentions and find ourselves judging the situation and wondering what we can do about all that is supposedly wrong with this world. We easily become trapped in the right/wrong and good/bad thinking.

Seeing from the right or wrong, good or bad perspective forces us to fix what we can and often causes us

155

to feel hopeless in the situations that are out of our control. Hopelessness can easily lead to feelings of separation and often throws us into a downward spiral of negativity that effects many other areas of our lives.

The black and white thinking we find ourselves in is not reserved for the global climate and many times can be found in our relationships. When we practice this thinking with our partner, the perception of one thing wrong or bad about our partner can cast a dark shadow over everything they do and everything they are.

This occurs when we perceive the opinions of our partner that differ from ours as broken or wrong. When we translate an action or the words of our partner as broken or wrong, we also see our partners as wrong or broken. We are judging the person, thing or situation as less than, unworthy, lacking, bad and many other negative definitions. From our egoic mind, we decide we must fix or correct them and from our fix-it mentality, we discover more that we feel needs to be fixed.

Fix Nothing; Transform Everything. Transforming is not about fixing it. While we can often take a negative situation and transform it into something that serves greater good, transforming is about creating paradigm shifts within our own hearts and minds.

A beautiful example of this occurred within me in 1994 when I was able to transform my feelings and inner dialogue around my son's passing three years earlier. I moved from deep anger, hopelessness, sadness and turmoil to a life of purpose and love. While I still wish he was here with me every day, I opened awareness to the pain, found understanding and acceptance and transformed my anger to passion, my hopelessness to faith, my sadness to joy, and my turmoil to purpose. It was not about fixing all those horrible feelings. It was not about fixing the cause of his death. It was in adopting new emotions that served me and opened me to greater understanding of purpose that the negative emotions faded. I have served far greater good since the transformation that I ever could have in my anger and sadness.

With no exceptions, every situation can be transformed. It is just not always the situation itself; it is more times than not, our perception of the situation that can transform. And, there is always greater peace and joy available in transforming self than there is in transforming the situation.

The first thing we must transform in any situation that does not serve greater good for us, our partners or our relationship is to transform our way of interpreting that which does not serve. Instead of seeing something as broken, wrong, or any of the other negative translations, we can choose instead to see that thing as not working for highest good. Instead of judging the person, we can transform our perception of them.

Many of the disagreements we have in our relationships are simply a difference of opinion. This does not need to translate into right or wrong. What one person sees as entertaining, may be seen by another as educational; neither is wrong, just different. What one person sees as easy may be seen by another as difficult. Again, a difference of opinion.

When we can determine that a difference of opinion is what is driving our need to fix something, we can seek understanding and acceptance of the situation instead. We can allow the difference to be a catalyst for learning, a resource. We do not need to change our opinion or the opinion of others to find understanding and acceptance.

Allowing the differing opinions to exist without judgment adds color and excitement to our life experience as the invitation to see a broader picture is given.

While many things are merely a difference of opinion, there are some situations, actions and words in our relationships that do not work to serve highest good, and there is absolutely no reason to continue tolerating those things as they are. To transform instead of fix is vital to extending happiness and love in the relationship. Transforming allows peace to exist and grow throughout the transformation process while fixing creates stress and chaos, hurt feelings and sometimes anger.

To fix that thing requires attention, intention and energy. When we give anything great attention, the feelings we have about it expand. If that thing is the perceived wrong or bad situation, we fall into the trap of fighting dark with dark. When we give that thing our energy, we expand that which we do not want. What we resist persists. Our focus on something we deem as wrong, broken or unworthy creates more of the same.

We are truly unable to fix anything, except for something material; mechanical. Looking back over the times we thought we fixed something, we can see that we simply transformed that thing or situation. When it comes to relationships and emotions, we can only transform and sometimes the only transformation is our perceptions and beliefs. We can transform that which does not serve us by seeing it in new light. We can assist our partners in the transformation process by sharing our new perceptions and inviting them to seek transformation for that which does not serve them. We must remember, though, it is totally our partner's responsibility to transform what they may be experiencing or feeling. Transformation of anything is an internal process.

In transforming our perceptions, we open opportunity to find understanding. Transformation provides us the means to remain loving and emotionally healthy no matter what we are dealing with in the relationship.

The tool, Fix Nothing; Transform Everything is not about ignoring or denying the perceived problems and it is not about repairing the situation or circumstance. From every situation, working or not working, serving or not serving, we can learn, we can grow, and we can transform.

To transform something that is not working in our relationship, we simply shift our energy to the feelings we desire and away from the negative ones we have been giving to the situation. By opening awareness to the issue or circumstance, we create opportunities that allow us to determine what we would prefer instead. It may be the total opposite of how we have been reacting to and thinking about the situation, or it could just be an adjustment that serves the greater well-being of ourselves, our partner or the relationship.

When we create a new dynamic; a new energy, around the situation we change our response to the situation. This shift in energy requires us to release what we do not want and replace it with the energy we desire. This release may be the letting go of the situation all together or it may be the release of our feelings about it. In this shift, we embrace new empowered and loving feelings towards the situation and everyone involved.

In some situations, we may believe our partner must make a shift. We see the transformation that is needed as their responsibility. While a transformation within our partner may be a beautiful resolution, we must remember,

159

an energetic shift from within ourselves offers tremendous healing as well. The transformation of the situation we experience within may very well be the invitation our partner needs to seek transformation for themselves.

Giving love instead of fixing or forcing change creates an energy that attracts transformation. We serve this transformation well when we do not harp on the negativity of the situation, and instead, communicate what we desire. Adding love, whether the situation changes or not, gifts us the ability to see our partner as more important than the issue. It allows us to experience and express love and peace in the situation, and ultimately, we elevate love and peace throughout our experience of the relationship and life.

In our relationships and in all we do, we serve highest good and well-being for all involved when we add love. Opening awareness to what we desire instead of intently focusing on that which is not working leads to transformation and it is here where we truly heal.

Elevate and Expand Your Relationship

Create new Behaviors and Expressions of Love

Elevate Your Expression of Love

As time goes on in our relationships, we tend to take the relationship, our partners and our part in the partnership for granted. It becomes easy for us to sit back and glide along when things are going smoothly. We often forget to elevate love which translates to allowing the relationship to grow stagnate and shrink. The Universe and all that is in it either expand with new growth or shrink from lack of growth. Relationships on all levels, especially intimate ones, abide by this natural law, as well.

Relationships, like all life experience have a Comfort Zone. The name itself explains what this is. We become comfortable and decide to not rock the boat. "If it ain't broke, don't fix it," is a perfect example of the belief systems many of us adopt throughout our lives and our relationships. With this philosophy though, boredom sets in, and the relationship begins to shrink. We begin to see what is not working and begin looking for ways to fix it. If we cannot fix it, many people decide their relationship is broken beyond repair and look for ways to bail out.

The methods we choose to fix our relationship sometimes work; often they do not and only increase the perception of brokenness. Sadness, loneliness and feelings of failure set in and we seek other ways to fix the relationship when elevating love is the greatest thing we can do to resolve all we perceive as broken.

When we express love into our relationship, we elevate and expand it. As we turn our focus away from the perceived problems and focus on hope, we see opportunity to grow the relationship and find deeper goodness and love. In the beginning of our relationship, we are focused on the love and the happiness available there. Initially, curiosity and a desire to grow the relationship keep our attention and intention on our partner and the love we have together.

The good news is that this state of awareness is not reserved for those first few months. With conscious attention, we can enjoy this state of awareness throughout the entire relationship. In this state of awareness, we can overcome all that may not be perfect, even if we have been with our partner for years. This state of awareness opens us to experience greater love, appreciation and peace.

When "the honeymoon is over" we allow our intention and attention to waver, and it is here the judgments and comparisons begin scratching at the edges of our love and happiness. Who says the honeymoon needs to be over? We can continually discover new things about our partner even after years of being together. Our partner, like ourselves, is continuously evolving, and when we add love into that evolution, we can appreciate and even be grateful for the expansion of the person we see.

It is when we see through the eyes of our ego, instead of the eyes of our heart, that seemingly insurmountable problems often arise. We begin to see the relationship as a "me against them" situation, when in truth, the relationship remains an opportunity for connected growth when we simply elevate our expression of love.

Elevating the love we express does not mean we must do more things. It is not that we raise the number of chores we do in hopes of greater appreciation from our partner. It is not that we increase the number of times each day that we say, "I Love You." We simply elevate the expression of love in the things we already do and say. Of course, if there are areas in the relationship where we are withholding love, we can adjust there and begin expressing love into them. We can see each situation through the eyes of love. We can more deeply express love in our words, the way we look at our partner and the energy we give into the relationship.

Some key questions we can ask ourselves that will assist in determining how to elevate our expression of love are:

> What can I change or transform now that allows me to elevate the love I express into the relationship?
> What part of me can I transform from a place of withholding love to one of radiating love?
> How can I express love more deeply in the ways I already show love?
> What are ways I can express purest love even if I receive no response from my partner?
> What areas of my relationship am I receiving love that I do not fully appreciate?

While this may appear to be adding more to an already busy schedule, it will quickly become second nature, and our expression of love will naturally elevate. As we shift our intention to ways we can express love more deeply, the worries and concerns over those things that are not-working begin to fade, and the time we once spent in worry now becomes time we spend in love.

Every expression of love we offer comes back to us in abundance; even if the love we receive is coming from ourselves. The act of expressing love is in and of itself, a loving gift we give ourselves. As we express and receive love, we find love is more plentiful and abundant throughout our lives.

It is important to our own well-being to stay clear of comparing the amount of love we give into the relationship to that which our partner gives. The love we give is not a competition with our partner. We are not keeping a score card tallying who gives more. We cheat ourselves and the relationship when we compare. We cheat ourselves of giving the love we have within to give.

This competitive state of mind causes us to hold back what we give and eventually we will find we have nothing left to offer. The love we hoard and hold within our own hearts will shrivel up and blow away. Love is meant to share, and in sharing, we receive. Even if we are the only person in the relationship willing to participate and practice this tool, love elevates within us and radiates from us. The law of attraction shows us that what we energetically put out into the world will return to us abundantly.

This holds true in our relationship, as well. What we do to elevate our expression of love into the relationship will come back to us. When we release expectations of how that will look, we receive. Releasing expectations of where and from whom love comes, we are open to receive love more fully. The love we see returning to us may not be from our partner in the beginning. It may be from sources outside of our intimate relationship; however, continued elevation of the love we express will eventually radiate so fully with our partner, a foundation is created where they will be invited to respond in kind.

While there are no promises that our partner will elevate their own expression of love, we still receive the benefits of the love we express. We can choose to be a beacon of loving light into our relationship. We can choose to express love instead of withholding it. Withholding love shrinks our own experience of the relationship, expressing love elevates our experience.

We have a choice. Our partner also has a choice. However, the choice to elevate our expression of love does need not be reliant on our partner's choice. When they choose to join us in elevating the love they express, love more fully radiates throughout the relationship and life. If they choose to withhold love, love still radiates in our life and our experience of the relationship. Even if the relationship ends, we can choose to elevate our expression of love into the remnants of the relationship and experience authentic love.

What we experience is reliant on our own perceptions and expressions. As we elevate our expression of love, we elevate our experience of love. We choose our experience just as we choose our expression.

Choose To be Happy
Rather Than Right

What is more important: to be happy or to be right? When we are honest with ourselves, we will find this is not an easy question to answer. Approaching this question with our minds often determines being right as most important. Answering with our hearts, we choose happiness.

Contrary to popular belief, happiness is not reliant on being right. We do not have to be right to be happy. Happiness stands on its own, and we can choose it in every situation we face and in every moment of our lives. Being right will rarely get us to authentic happiness. On the other hand, when we choose to be happy first, we create an environment where we feel that all is right. Even when our position on a topic can be proven wrong, happiness can carry us through. Choosing happy moves right and wrong thinking into a much less important position and we will feel as if all is well.

When we choose to pursue being right first, happiness can be quite elusive and can even seem to move further and further from our reach. It is not winning an argument that offers continued happiness. Everything does not need to go our way before we can be happy.

I once worked with a group who totally agreed with me when I said choose to be happy rather than right. Or so they thought. The moment I completed my presentation of a new challenge for them, they began putting together a list of things to do so they could be right which they thought would lead them to the happiness available upon completion of the challenge. This thinking led them to argument over the "right" way to proceed; it left some people ignored and the progress made in the challenge was minor at best.

It took some doing to help them understand how to reverse their thinking. We began again, this time choosing happiness first and the task of completing the challenge became fun, less daunting and the progress they made was amazing. Everyone in the group was included, laughter replaced bickering and ideas were shared by nearly every member of the group. Once the group completed the challenge, they realized how being happy throughout the process allowed them to find solutions that were right for them.

Our relationships are the same. We often have a list of things that we believe need to be certain ways before happiness can occur. Even when we take all the right steps and reach the right destination, we are not assured happiness. The situations where right takes precedence over happy will be a struggle and love is placed on the sidelines. This will never lead to happiness. We must simply choose to be happy. Be happy first. Once we choose happiness, we make happiness our intention and it becomes our top priority. And, isn't it more fun to be happy?

When we choose right mentality over happiness we must remember that to be right, someone or something must be wrong. While that may not seem like too big of a concern, we can each reflect on a moment where our opinions or ideas were considered wrong. Even in the minor things, being made to feel wrong never promotes happiness. When we consistently strive to be right, in other words, make our partner wrong, we will drive a wedge between us and our partner; our relationship will suffer; sometimes greatly.

It is not always someone else we are proving wrong. We also accuse ourselves of being wrong. We can all recall a time or two when we considered ourselves wrong about a decision we made, a step we took, a project we joined, and so on. Whether the accusation of being wrong comes from outside of us or from within, it does not feel good, and certainly not happy.

We can flip our way of thinking around and choose happy. To be happy, we need only choose it and most of the time when we choose happy, the people around us become a bit happier too; or at least less angry, sad, stressed, etc. When we choose happy, our environment seems lighter, more peaceful, more comfortable. When we choose happy, our attitude about all things lifts to a more positive place. When we choose happy, wrong seems further away and right is just not as important.

Now this is not an invitation to abandon our morals or ethics. It is not saying to toss our values out the window. What this tool encourages us to do is to walk an enlightened path which allows life to become much easier and more effortless. Choosing happy allows us to choose what resonates within our hearts and allows that to be our expression to the world.

Choosing happy is a personal choice; it requires nothing from anyone else. We do not have to rely on our significant other to do anything differently. We do not need specific circumstance to line up before happiness is available. Our happiness is our choice. Happiness does not occur because of something outside of us. Sure, if someone gives us a new car, we will be happy for a while, but happiness that is reliant or caused by something outside of us is temporary at best. Authentic happiness is an internal choice.

We all know how wonderful it feels to be happy, yet we still seem to shift back to our need to be right. Even though we feel the benefits of being happy and even though we understand that happiness can shift our experience of anything to one that is enjoyable, pleasant, empowering and all sorts of other positive experiences, we still tend to revert to our need to be right. To choose happiness regularly, we must create a conscious practice of choosing happiness. We also must understand some of the reasons we slide back to being right.

One reason is that we attach our happiness to things outside of us: material things, people, experiences. Those can bring us happiness but when our happiness is attached to those things, as soon as the new wears off, they get old, damaged or go away, we lose our happiness. If we believe that happiness will only come once we have possession of something, happiness will be absent until we get those things. When we lose happiness, or it does not come to us as hoped, we try to make since out of life by justifying, which easily moves to judging, which opens the door to right/wrong thinking.

Another reason we turn back to being right is our EGO. Yep that lovely little nuisance that resides within. It is that part of us that takes fear and elevates it. Ego tells us that we must prove we are right or we will be wrong. Ego tells us, and quite convincingly, that there is only one right and we cannot begin to be happy until we are right.

We often fall into the belief system that every aspect about something must be right or wrong. When we perceive one small detail of something as wrong, we consider the whole thing wrong. Look at the political climate these days.

Each party claims the other to be wrong and any idea from the opposing party is disregarded because of its source. Unfortunately, much of society has bought into this rhetoric and we are seeing a divide in our country and our world like never before.

As a society, we have forgotten that there can be many so-called right ways to perceive or experience any situation. Earlier we looked at the definition of the statement, "They were tight." I listed several common answers. Each answer is correct, none are wrong; however, we can easily perceive a differing definition as wrong, and in turn, perceive the person offering that definition as wrong. Once we perceive someone as wrong, we can easily begin to see everything about that person as wrong. Nearly every situation or circumstance in life contains multiple "right" solutions and options.

We have proven that we can move beyond right and wrong thinking in many things. Fashion, car styles, music, diets, and many other examples exist where we allow others their own preferences without considering them wrong.

Even though we have progressed in many areas, we still have many influences attempting to drag us back into right/wrong thinking. The market place is a powerful example. The ads for many products tell us they are the right choice, and some go so far as to show us their competitors and claim they are the wrong choice. We are assaulted with right or wrong thinking everywhere we look, so it is not so surprising that we fall into that mindset as often as we do.

While it is a bit easier to steer clear of right/wrong thinking when considering automobiles or clothes, it is difficult when a situation affects us on the personal level. Being right becomes quite a bit more important when we are personally affected. Anytime an opposing opinion appears to contradict our opinion, our ego stands up and says, "Whoa, wait a minute..."

Ego sends us into fight or flight mode. Ego tells us that since the other person is claiming themselves to be right, they must be claiming that we are wrong. Ego tells us we must fight to be right. And the battle begins. Ego does not look for a place where both people can be right. Ego does not look for compromise. Ego wants us to prove we are right and it does not stop there. Ego demands we force someone to move from their position to ours. In the process of fighting our battle, we are saying to the other person, "You are wrong, I am right, come join me." Some of these interactions can become heated and frightening. Many relationships have ended because of right/wrong thinking.

One example is a guy who insisted empty clothes hangers be put in a certain spot in the closet. He expected his wife to do the same. She did not consider it a high priority and usually left her empty hangers mixed in with other clothes. He was determined to prove his way right and continually claimed she was wrong. She tired of the constant criticism and being made wrong; their marriage ended.

Another example is a guy whose best friend was his dog. This dog went everywhere with him. Even on dates to very nice places with his girlfriend, the dog went with them. The dog did stay in the car while they went into the restaurants, only because of laws, but the dog still went everywhere this guy went. The dog sat between the man and his date while riding in the car, at home of the sofa, and even slept between them. Instead of seeking understanding of his girlfriend's objection to this issue, he saw her as wrong and often accused her of being wrong about it all. Tired of consistently being made wrong, she ended the relationship.

In each of these scenarios, there were so many ways to find common ground, to communicate and come to solution. There was space to compromise and some give and take would have helped tremendously. Choosing happiness instead of right would have eased the tension and allowed for solutions to be found. The need to be right prevented any of that from happening.

Just like these examples, needing to be right stops us in so many ways. Ego combined with pride prevented these two guys from seeing anything but their "right" way. Now girls, just because I used guys in these examples, do not for one-minute think women do not do this as well. We all do it and unfortunately, we do it often. Some instances are more extreme and noticeable than others, but we do it often. No matter how we handle the situation when it arises, when we fall into the need to be right and allow it to play out, we are trying to make the other person wrong.

Earlier I mentioned that we do not have to have everything going our way to be happy. Happiness really is a choice, so how do we make that choice in times where we really feel strongly about something. Choosing to be happy always falls into the self-awareness category. To choose happiness, we must open our awareness to our feelings in the moment. We must be aware that the need to be right has surfaced again. We must be aware of the situation, and we must be fully aware that we do have choices, and those choices can be true and authentic and offer peace to a situation.

There are some situations that carry great importance and we feel we must make a stand. For me, some of the situations I feel are important enough to take a stand in support of are the rights of people in general. Women's rights, civil rights, children's rights are examples. I believe

173

people's right to be happy, their right to live according to their beliefs, and their right to love and be loved are non-negotiable. And I believe these things are right. I also believe I can remain loving and peaceful and happy as I stand in support of these things.

Each of us must decide what is a non-negotiable in our relationship. To do that requires checking in and becoming aware of why something is important and just how important it is. When we determine the true importance of something we can determine the available options. We can then determine how we can hold true to our cause and remain happy while doing so. Being happy is way more important than being right in every aspect of life.

William Shakespeare, in Romeo and Juliet, Act 2 Scene 2, said, a rose by any other name still smells as sweet. The same is true for the situations we experience. Whether we call our point of view right or wrong, the situation is the same. If we fight to win someone over to our side, it merely changes the number of people calling the situation right or wrong. The situation does not change until we drop the label and shift our energy about it.

When we choose happiness as our default emotion, the need to be right shows up less and less and that is a very peaceful and loving and kind place to be. We can allow happiness and love to be the primary energy in our relationship and we can release right/wrong thinking. When we choose love and happiness, all things will be well.

Express Gratitude

Other than expressing love and choosing happiness, one of the greatest things we can bring into our relationship is gratitude. Meister Eckhart said that if the only prayer we ever say in our entire life is thank you, it will be enough.

When was the last time you stopped right where you were, looked around, and said "Thank You"? When we begin to take life and our relationships for granted, we tend to see only that which we interpret as wrong. Unless we are highly enlightened people, we focus on the wrongness and the result is, either subliminally or openly, communicating to our partner that things are not working. The result of this communication, in our partner's belief, easily becomes that they are wrong. To transform the situation, we must move our attention to what is working, what is elevating the relationship; we must embrace gratitude.

In all of life, what we hold in gratitude expands and elevates. When we express gratitude, more comes to us for which to be grateful. This is especially true in relationships. When we hold our relationship in gratitude, when we express gratitude, we expand the relationship, lift our partner, and enrich our own experience. While there may be areas of the relationship we do not hold in gratitude, even if we cannot hold the entirety of our relationship in gratitude, there are some parts of the relationship or moments in our relationship that are worthy of gratitude. And it is in these glimpses of light, we can build and enrich our experience of gratitude in the relationship.

175

We begin by looking more deeply at our partner. Finding something about our partner to hold in gratitude allows us to see more about them that is gratitude worthy, and then we expand on that by holding it in gratitude, feeling the gratitude and expressing gratitude.

Seeing the love they express, even if it is merely a spark of affection, is a beautiful acknowledgement of the love available always. Embrace that love with gratitude. Seeing the intention behind their actions and holding the intention in gratitude opens the door to deeper love.

It is easy for our focus to become glued to the things that are not working to elevate love. The things that do not serve the relationship can often consume our awareness. We can shift our attention, though, and it requires dedicated practice to move from the fear of things going wrong to the possibility of things being wonderful. Expanding the gratitude we hold for our partner keeps our focus on what is truly important in the relationship, love. Holding our partner in gratitude shifts the energy we express into the relationship and love elevates.

Next, we turn our gratitude to the relationship itself. Seeking ways the relationship serves as a vehicle for love and holding these in gratitude, we open our awareness to the love and comfort there. When we can be grateful for all the relationship offers, we expand our experience of gratitude and find more that is gratitude worthy.

We also turn our focus to all that we hold in gratitude about ourselves. While this practice is beneficial throughout all of life, in a relationship, gratitude for self opens us to see the beauty of the loving expressions we bring. In gratitude, ego is silenced as ego cannot exist where love is present. When we see the goodness we share, we expand the love we offer.

Beginning a gratitude practice is a loving way to consider, explore and elevate gratitude in the relationship. There are many ways to practice gratitude and here are a few to consider:

Gratitude Practice 1

"The Gratitude List." Take time before going to sleep at night to express three or more things for which you are grateful. Of those three nightly items, express at least one pertaining to the relationship. This is not necessarily a quest for those things in the deepest levels of your being. This practice does not need to be difficult. While those deeply meaningful things can certainly be part of your list, gratitude even for the smallest and seemingly insignificant things expand your gratitude as well.

You can begin with expressing gratitude for the relationship you are in, the air you breathe, the roof over your head, the survival of another day. You can include your family, pets, friends. There is no limit in this practice, simply list three or more things each evening that you can hold in gratitude. Once something makes it to your list, focus on it and feel deep gratitude for it. Feeling gratitude in your heart for that which you list, expands the gratitude you have for that thing, and you create an emotional magnet drawing more into your life for which to be grateful.

With this gratitude practice, you empower your ability to experience and express gratitude when you add new things each night. Only repeat an item on your list when you wish to feel deeper gratitude for it. Expanding the list expands your experience of gratitude and that in turn expands your expression of gratitude.

Gratitude Practice 2

Another practice is to take time each day to pray gratitude over life. "Praying gratitude" is not to be confused with "praying for gratitude." The word "for" places our focus squarely on our perceived lack of that thing. When we pray gratitude over something, we hold the entirety of that thing in gratitude, even if we do not fully understand or appreciate each component of the thing in that moment.

You can extend this into a prayer of gratitude for all of life. Holding all of life in gratitude allows even the seemingly negative or dark things of life an opportunity to transform into something you can truly hold in gratitude. Gratitude encourages you to look beyond the negative and see love. Gratitude invites you to see truth, beyond the surface emotions you may attach to a person or situation, and it is here you find deeper love, forgiveness, healing and rest. Gratitude transforms your experience of life and moves you from fear to love.

Praying Gratitude allows you to understand that all things in life can be a blessing. You can see that everything in life has a purpose, a meaning or a lesson. Even those things you may perceive in your relationship as "bad" can transform into something that serves the highest good of the relationship, your partner and you. When you hold gratitude for all things, you receive an opportunity to transform, to feel healing and to expand your experience of goodness and love.

Gratitude Practice 3

Another practice is "Be Mindfully Grateful." While finding gratitude in the small things allows you to bring gratitude more fully into your life, this practice is about being fully present in gratitude, always. When you are fully present, everything has value, and everything deserves your gratitude. The things you withhold from your gratitude are products of your inner fear. When fear is present, you are not. Fear is "Future Events Appearing Real" or "False Evidence Appearing Real." Fear is an illusion created by your incredible mind pointing out the things that might go wrong if you take a step. Fear makes the things that might happen look real. Fear tends to overpower the part of your mind that asks, "How incredibly cool and awesome will it be when I take that step."

There are only two natural fears; the fear of loud noises and the fear of falling. All other fears have been learned, and if you can learn those fears, you can unlearn them. When you bring your gratitude practice into present moment, when you are fully mindful in your practice, fear is silenced. You must release the habit of waiting on something to come to you before you can be grateful. Right now, in this moment, there is so much to be grateful for. Right now, in this moment, feel gratitude.

Gratitude Practice 4

Another practice is called "The Gratitude Walk." A gratitude bike ride or a gratitude sitting; or any other activity allowing for complete presence and mindfulness will work just as well. I want to share with you how I practice this;

however, it can be adjusted to suit any activity. I have a two-mile route that I walk while doing this. I arm myself with a beautiful 108 bead Mala that a dear friend made for me. As I walk I meditate on gratitude. I begin my walk and hold one of the beads between my thumb and middle finger. I pray gratitude over something in the present, something in that very moment. I move to the next bead and do the same thing. Each expression of gratitude is focused on something in that very moment. This two-mile trip allows me to go through the Mala at least twice. (*Note- The mala is not necessary; it simply works as a reminder to stay present*)

Now, here is the challenging part, I do not repeat anything. This brings into my awareness a minimum of two-hundred and sixteen things I hold in gratitude; all in the present moment. This may seem impossible and I must admit, when I got to around bead forty on my first gratitude walk, I began thinking I had set myself up for failure. But the coolest thing happened, when I could not find anything else in sight for which to be grateful, I heard a hawk. I began expressing gratitude for things I heard. I then expressed gratitude for the things I felt, and suddenly, I was able to see, hear and feel even more for which to be grateful. The key? Be present.

This practice can be done in the middle of the living room. You can sit in stillness, become mindful of all that surrounds you and begin expressing gratitude. You can focus on your relationship, your home, your family and even more. Opening awareness to the present moment reveals the abundance of gratitude worthy things available in your life.

Gratitude adds tremendous value in our lives. We see more value in ourselves. This mindful gratitude elevates our attitude, patience and understanding. It elevates our

180

willingness and guides us to take a step into areas we once shied away from. For me this practice is as much about being fully present as it is about being grateful. The combination of the two is a powerful duo.

Becoming present and adding gratitude to our relationship allows us to see more beauty, purpose and goodness. We have so much to be grateful for. As we expand our gratitude, our outlook on life in general lifts and brings our attitude to much higher levels. We lift our self-esteem and our self-worth as well. We cannot have low self-esteem or feelings of low self-worth while holding all of life in gratitude.

When a gratitude practice becomes difficult due to life situations, we must simply look within to our heart. Allow feelings of love to begin and hold that feeling in gratitude. We allow gratitude to expand by seeing more through eyes of love. We elevate our relationship by seeing our partner, our self and the relationship with love and hold it all in gratitude.

Set Intentions with Your Partner

Throughout this book, we have done much work to open awareness of our relationship and our expressions into it. This chapter is about taking that awareness much further. It is in awareness that we can truly see and understand what we want on the heart level, the level of our essence. It is on this level we elevate our expression and experience of love.

Through awareness we can see the illusions our ego has set in place for what they truly are, illusions. With awareness, fear subsides and hope rises.

It is with intentions we begin manifesting the relationship we desire. The first part of this tool does not require the participation from our partner as it is vitally important we create intentions of our own. Once we create and set an intention, the energy we experience and express will shift more deeply into love. Of course, if your partner is willing to participate and create their own intentions, the energy shift will be even more dynamic.

To begin, we must consider those things we discovered that are working and the things that are not working in the relationship. We are leaving judgments and comparisons out of this process just as we are learning to do in our relationships and lives.

Begin with consideration of the things that do not work in the relationship. Consider what needs to happen with them. Typically, we either want them to go away or we want them to transform. What is important with either scenario is that we believe a positive shift will take its place.

With intention setting, we release our focus on what is not working and see the positive replacement. We see and focus on what we desire, and we create a clear mental picture of what this is.

Next, we consider the things that are working in the relationship and consider how we can elevate these things. How can we give more love into them? How can we express more of our hearts into these things? How can we expand these things even further?

We find our answers through visioning. When we vision these things, we see how they fit into our relationship. We vision our ideal relationship and see how these things add to the perfection we desire. If, in our vision, something seems to take away from the happiness and love of the relationship, we let them go. Those things that add value, love and joy into the relationship, we embrace them more deeply in the vision.

We move beyond our thinking mind and allow our heart to be a part of the vision. The heart mind connection is called wholeheartedness, and it is from this place within that we vision. In our vision, we truly see the relationship, our partner, ourselves as we desire them to be. We feel the feelings associated with the desired relationship on the heart level. We hear the words associated with a desired relationship abundant with love. We can even go so far as to smell things associated with an ideal relationship.

See it. Feel it. Hear it. Smell it

We must keep in mind that this is not a comparison to someone else's relationship, this is our own vision, and there are no right or wrong ways to vision the elevated experience of love this brings.

As our vision becomes clear, we move it into the present moment. We vision it as already in existence. We see it, feel it, hear it, smell it as if it already exists, right here, right now. We can spend time here just taking it all in, embracing it. As we see, hear, feel and smell this newly elevated and expanded relationship in our vision, we experience it.

What we experience in our vision is real. The feelings we feel in this process are not imagined. When we align with our vision, we feel the actual feelings associated with our ideal relationship. These feelings are beautiful resources of support as we move into the next step and beyond.

Once we have a clear vision of our ideal relationship, we begin setting intentions that align with our vision. We ask of ourselves, "What can I do right now to achieve this feeling? What can I adjust to manifest the sights I see in my vision? What can I say to speak into the relationship these things I hear in my vision? How can I create the smells associated with my vision of the perfect relationship?"

We ask these questions and any others that solicit the answers we seek, and we listen for answers. When we become still in our minds, we will hear. Once we receive our answers, in full or in part, we set intentions to do, say, feel or experience our vision in this present moment.

It is important to set intentions that are not conditional or dependent on other people, even our partner. The intentions we set are personal, and we alone can manifest the outcomes we desire.

Setting intentions allows for movement. Once we set intentions and begin our path to that which we desire, we have an emotional GPS that lets us know when we are taking a step that does not resonate with our intention. We can tell when something is working or not working by our feelings, and we can adjust when necessary. When we set intentions and monitor our progress along the way, we become aware of bigger and better versions of our intentions.

Each one of us has our own vision of an ideal relationship and it is vital that we understand what that is for us. Once we are clear on our vision, we can share with our partner what we experienced. They too can share with us, and it serves both of us to find complete understanding of each other's visions before moving on. Once we understand, whether we agree or not, together we move to the next part of the process which is vision together.

(If your partner has not been participating in this journey so far, ask them if they are willing to vision with you about your relationship. If they are, ask them if they would be willing to take time to vision their own perfect relationship before you begin. If they will not, no worries, this step can still be enlightening and powerful for you, your partner and your relationship.)

When visioning with our partner, we obviously must communicate with each other. Since we are communicating with our partner, we are tempted to vision from our mind and block out our heart. This poses a challenge for us as being in our mind will only lead us to ideas. While those ideas may seem like part of our vision, being in our head removes our heart from the equation which prevents us from truly and completely experiencing our vision. We must wholeheartedly participate to vision.

To begin, agree to vision the relationship as it serves highest good and breathe together. We each begin a gentle rhythmic breathing; breathing in we know we are breathing in; breathing out, we know we are breathing out. Once connected with our own heart, we open our eyes and look deeply into the eyes of our partner and connect to their heart. We can deepen our heart connection by placing our right hand over our heart throughout the visioning.

Once connected on the heart level, we bring into focus a relationship that is loving and peaceful, and whatever else serves highest good. From here, we either go into silence and see a clear picture within our own heart and mind, then share what we experience, or we can simply discus it together while in a state of visioning; sharing what we see, hear, feel, as if it is already done. This is not a place for right or wrong thinking. This is sharing and allowing our own vision to expand while our partner's vision expands.

Once we have created a vision that resonates with us both, we can set intentions that align with our vision.

We then continue the process by bringing in specific areas of focus for the relationship and repeating the process of visioning and setting intentions.

Focusing, first, on the areas where our individual visions are already in alignment creates a platform that allows us to vision any areas where we may not be in alignment. When addressing areas that are not working in the relationship, we vision for what we desire in its place and allow the thing that is not working to fade away.

As we vision with our partner, we can talk about the good things we desire that may not be present. We can talk about the things we desire to expand and elevate. Throughout the intention setting portion of the process, we ask questions to gain clarity and understanding. When asking questions, we ask open ended questions and then listen with the intent to understand.

There may be some areas where no common vision can be found. We still have options. We can come back to it later. We can consider adopting one idea or the other. We can allow the difference to remain and consider how we can both grow from it. Whichever consideration fits, create a vision around it, be clear on how it works for the betterment of the relationship, and set intentions together that serve the relationship.

Set intentions together. Again, this is not a time to argue or see each other as right or wrong. This is a time to vision for the relationship of our desires. We embrace sameness and differences alike and give each other room to be authentic and unique. As mentioned earlier in this book, the differences sometimes create an atmosphere for growth, they can open us to appreciation of our partner's authenticity.

Love Is a Verb

Love is far more than a four-letter word that we toss over our shoulder as we head out the door. It is more than a half-hearted response to someone else's expression of love. Love is a feeling that rises from deep within our souls. It is an experience and an expression. In other words; it is a verb; it is action.

Many of us consider our loving actions to be on the physical level, and while many of those actions do express love, the actions that most sincerely express love are of the emotional and spiritual nature. Gifts in the form of roses, candy and cards, dinners and dates, foot and neck massages, and many other actions or gifts are wonderful to give and receive; however, it is the loving intention behind those actions and gifts that hold the most meaning and this intention can be applied to anything we do within the relationship.

Being fully present and feeling loving gratitude for our partner lifts the presence of love in the relationship. Listening with the intent to understand carries far more meaning than any attempt to seek resolution of an issue. "Love is a Verb" simply means we connect on the heart level. We lovingly connect with our partner through our actions, and our expressions.

To fully understand love as a verb, we must look at the difference between "being in love" with our partner and "loving" them.

To be in love with someone is a passive acceptance of the love we feel towards and from that person. There is certainly nothing wrong with this unless it is the only experience of love we have in the relationship. Being in love relies heavily on what our partner has to offer. As we wait for the other person's offerings, we can easily become discouraged and begin focusing on what we may perceive as shortcomings. These perceptions quickly jade our beliefs about them. When "in love" is the foundation of our relationship, as time passes, we can begin to perceive no expression of love from our partner. We can begin to see the person we fell in love with as unwilling to offer any expression of love.

Using love as a verb, we no longer wait for love to come to us. We express love into the relationship. We see our partner in the light of love. We experience their presence with love. The love we have within for that person is shown through our actions, even if the only action we take is holding them in the love found in our heart. When we love someone, we express love. We experience respect and joy radiating from our hearts, throughout our entire body and outwardly. This love is expressed whether we use words or not. In this expression we create an environment rich with love and much of that love comes back to us in many ways whether it be from our partner or our own loving feelings.

Love as a verb elevates and expands the relationship, while being in love with someone provides less opportunity for growth. Loving someone is our heart in action. From our heart we see goodness even in rough times. When love is a verb, we stand more confidently in our relationship and we are not as insecure when our partner forgets to kiss us good-bye as they leave for work or forgets an important date.

When we love someone, our beliefs about them stay healthier and more positive. When our beliefs about our partner are strong and loving, our expressions into the relationship and toward our partner will remain strong and loving in all we do. Our actions are greatly affected by the beliefs we carry within.

I was taught many years ago the value of beliefs and how they can truly change life. An earlier chapter in this book was dedicated to the tool, "Your Beliefs Create Your Reality." In this chapter, we expand on this truth as we focus on loving beliefs and thoughts. Our beliefs of love for our partner and our relationship create our reality and our expressions of love support and strengthen that reality.

To briefly summarize the earlier chapter, our thoughts are energy. This energy, when continued, creates our beliefs, and our beliefs create our reality. The energy we create with our thoughts is powerful. These energies not only have the power to create our own reality, they have the power to greatly affect the reality of others.

Our energetic field extends eight to twelve feet outside of our physical body, and this energy directly affects those around us. In each of my seminars, trainings and group events, I demonstrate how our beliefs are powerful enough to create other's realities as well as our own. In the hundreds of times I have used this demonstration, it has never failed. The energy that radiates from our bodies will never fail either. What we express energetically will determine what we experience.

When our thoughts are stuck on our partner being unloving, those thoughts become energy, then beliefs, and we create the reality of an unloving partner. When our thoughts are focused on our partner doing nothing to elevate love in the relationship, we come to believe it and our reality manifests a partner who will do nothing to elevate love. And if we think them to be doing harm to the relationship, we will begin to believe that they are doing harm, and our reality will become one where our relationship is damaged.

Conversely, when we see through eyes of love, when we think loving thoughts, we create loving beliefs and ultimately, we experience a loving reality. As we open awareness to our partner's expressions of love, no matter how huge or small they may be, we begin to believe our partner to be loving and we enrich the loving environment in our relationship.

To create this loving environment, we must first believe ourselves to be loving. We must open to the love we have within and see through eyes of love. We must think loving thoughts and in this, we create loving energy that radiates through us and from us. From this loving energy, we create loving beliefs; first for ourselves and then for our partner. As we turn more fully and genuinely to loving thoughts, we practice love as a verb. We mindfully embrace love within, and we express love out into the relationship.

The first expression of love we can express into our relationship is to shift any negative or fearful thoughts we have about our partner or the relationship. We shift from fear-based thoughts to thoughts of love. We can choose to see our partner and all they do with love. Even if we do not appreciate the things they do, we can wrap them with love and seek deeper understanding.

We elevate love by shifting our thinking. We create a more loving belief and we create a deeper and more loving reality.

Feel What They Feel

When we feel understood, we feel validated. Our partner is no different. One of the greatest gifts we can give our partner is to allow them time with their feelings. We may not understand the feelings they are experiencing and that is okay. The fact that we care enough to allow them time with their feelings is a wonderful gift.

Be cautious though, as it is tempting to ask, nag and maybe interrogate our partner in search of answers so we can fix what it is they are going through. To fix an issue or problem for our partner sends a message that we do not believe them capable of dealing with it on their own.

While giving our partner time with their own feelings is a beautiful gift, there are times where understanding of their feelings enrich the relationship. With understanding we can often offer greater support.

Before understanding of our partner's feelings can ever take place, we must let go of our interpretations and perceptions of what they may be going through. Every individual will deal with and feel situations differently. What we may think is an appropriate feeling in a specific situation may be completely different than what our partner feels appropriate. To suggest our feeling is best, serves only to de-value our partner's experience.

The truth of what is going on is this: no matter what they may be feeling, no matter how misguided or unreasonable it may appear to us, our partner is experiencing feelings for one reason or another and that is real to them which makes it real to us. We play no part in the healing process when we downplay, mimic, ignore or disregard what they are going through.

This does not mean we have to sit there and allow them to wallow in despair or fall into deep depression. Neither do we have to take on their feelings. The only purpose it serves when we take on their feelings is that we both fall into the darkness of despair with them. We cannot take the feelings away from our partner. We cannot feel the feelings for them. None of that works; however, we can support them when we seek understanding.

This is a great time for a disclaimer. If you feel that your partner is falling into a depression, do a little research on the symptoms of depression. If your concerns are still valid, discuss the possibilities of seeing a therapist with your partner. Do not force this issue unless they are not able to help themselves. Not all bad moods or negative outlooks on life are depression so be cautious with this. Do not attempt to be your partner's therapist, even if you are a therapist. Reach out to someone if need be. Most importantly, seek ways to assist them through the feelings. Avoidance on their part or numbing themselves to the feelings will never resolve the issue; it will only cover it up temporarily; allowing it to resurface at some other time, usually even stronger.

Okay, so you decided this is not something that needs professional help; perfect. *Disclaimer number two, keep an eye on things so you can reach out if need be. Just because your partner may not need a professional now does not mean they will not need one later. Just remain aware of where they are emotionally and encourage them to take steps that serve their well-being.*

This tool is helpful in realizing what our partner is going through and should be done in a very loving and gentle way. We will have to feel some of what they are going through if we really want to be effective in this process, but as mentioned earlier, we do not need to take on their feelings and own them. "Feel What They Feel" is about truly feeling and understanding our partner's feelings so we can support and console them while they are experiencing the feelings.

So here is the tool:

Imagine what it is your partner is feeling. Tune into what caused them to have the feelings. Do your best to understand what they are feeling and why. If the why is not evident, no worries, the feelings are most important. You do not have to wait for them to say something, just tap into how they feel. Whether perceived as good or bad, right or wrong, working or not-working, tap into what your partner feels.

This will be difficult to do at first as our tendency is to think something along the lines of, "If I were in your shoes, I would probably feel like... fill in the blank". The objective here is to think of how they are feeling based on their experience not how you would feel in their place. To add your feelings in the same circumstances cheats them of their feelings and cheats you out of understanding. While it is a gesture that lets them know you are trying, it is not nearly as powerful as working to fully understand them.

If you have been in the relationship for even a few weeks, you have enough knowledge about your partner to begin knowing how they will feel in a given situation. If you do not, now is the time to start learning. This is a great exercise to do that. Begin by imagining what you think they must feel. Take it deeper until you can feel that you tapped

194

into the real feelings. Feel it, know it and then at an appropriate time check in with your partner to verify. After checking in, if you are off by a mile or just slightly, ask your partner to help bring you more in alignment with their feelings.

This will help strengthen your connection; it will show them how much you really do care. While this tool will bring solutions into the light, the key is to feel what they feel. The greatest resource for healing emotions is to feel them until you no longer need to feel them. Allow your partner to have the time they need. When it is time to move forward, your understanding and validation provide support and a platform from which healing growth can occur.

The most important thing to remember here is that our partner has the right to have their feelings just as we have the right to have ours. This is not a way to judge the feelings or person as good or bad. This is just a way to understand and broaden awareness. We must remember - the greatest thing we can do is to fully understand without judgment what they are experiencing, and in doing this, we validate them.

Again, it is vital to remember, this is not a tool to "fix" our partner's feelings. This is simply a way to understand and let them know, they are not alone.

Smile Often - Hug Deeply

Smiling often and hugging deeply are two more ways to deepen the love in relationships and they cost us nothing. They can be done at anytime and anywhere, and they are expressions of authentic love to our partner. Offering a smile initiates a smile from others. Giving someone a hug opens their heart and ours more fully. Most importantly; both a smile and a hug deepen the happiness within our own hearts and expand our connection with others. As we give either of these, we too receive love.

Smile Often

It is impossible to feel fearful and dark emotions when we authentically smile from our heart. An authentic smile is more than an expression we place on our face for a moment or two. It is not the smile we sometimes plaster onto the façade we create to prevent others from seeing inside. An authentic smile is felt throughout our being and beyond.

An authentic smile manifests in our heart and radiates throughout our entire bodies and then is shared out into the world. This smile can be given in any moment of our lives no matter what situations we are experiencing. An authentic smile is conceived in our truth and opens pathways to the happiness in life we desire. This smile not only expresses as the upward curl of our lips, it radiates from our eyes and our entire aura, as well.

To smile this smile of the heart, we simply open awareness to the love that is within. Once judgments of right and wrong are removed from our focus, when we discontinue comparing our experience of life to the ways we are told it should be, and when we release expectations from others, we are free to look within, to our hearts. Surrendering all that does not serve love and happiness and focusing on truth, an authentic heartfelt smile is sure to come.

When we offer a heartfelt smile, we offer our greatest authenticity. Our authentic smile opens awareness of unconditional love throughout our lives and we open our heart to even more in life we can truly love. Our focus shifts from negative to positive, from chaos to peace, and we open more space within our hearts to embrace all that is loving. A smile illuminates compassion and kindness within and around us.

A smile on our face, especially when it begins in our heart, expands the beauty of our truth and even the beauty of our physical body. Smiles offer many benefits including:

- ➤ Improved mood
- ➤ Better relationships
- ➤ Lower blood pressure
- ➤ Stress relief
- ➤ Strengthened immune function
- ➤ Pain relief

Smiling often, when it is a smile of the heart, encourages happiness and love in our lives. Not only do we feel happier and more peaceful when we smile, the people around us feel happier and more peaceful. Providing a smile as our primary facial expression invites others to smile with us and the expression of love into this world is elevated exponentially.

Hug Deeply

A hug is also a beautiful gift which can be even more of an expression of the heart than a smile. While this gift delivers our heart expression to the receiver immediately, the gift also comes back to us immediately. As we give a hug, we also receive a hug. Even if the other person does not wrap their arms around us and squeeze, we receive the hug of their presence.

Before we get to far into this section, let's get clear on what a hug is not.

A hug is not what we see many athletes do when they come together, bump chests, wrap one arm around the other for a fraction of a second and walk away. A hug is not the type of hug that is sometimes called a granny hug where only shoulders touch and a brief pat on the back occurs. An authentic hug does not look like a teepee when seen from the side where only the sides of our face come near to the other person.

Hugging deeply is a full body embrace that lasts long enough to make a heart connection. This may be seconds, it may be minutes or even longer. An authentic hug embraces far more than the physical presence of another human being, it embraces their heart.

Hugging deeply is one of the purest forms of non-verbal communication. Volumes can be spoken through a hug without a word passing either person's lips. Speaking during a hug is certainly not forbidden, however, words sometimes distract from the deep level communication that can occur in a silent embrace.

When we hug, we open our hearts to be felt just as the person we are hugging opens theirs. Hugging deeply is not reserved for sensitive moments where we offer comfort. Hugs need not be saved for those moments before intimacy. While a heartfelt hug is appropriate for either of these instances, the hug can be used in many more situations. Some of the greatest videos on social media are those of people standing on busy streets with signs offering "Free Hugs."

The people receiving the free hugs feel loved even though they do not know the person offering hugs. The receivers' and givers' days are brightened. They release all the weight they have been carrying while embraced in the hug. These benefits of the hug are felt for much longer than the actual hug. The people receiving the hug carry that feeling with them throughout their day and very possibly for days to come. And often, the receiver of the hug shares a hug with someone else, thus, expanding the positive and loving energy of the initial hug.

In relationships, a hug is frequently one of those quick embraces given as couples go their own ways into their day. Hugs are sometimes given in times someone has had a bad day or after they have received troubling news. Intimate moments sometimes begin with hugs. The act of deeply hugging can be so much more than we allow it to be. Any time of the day or night is the perfect time to offer your partner a hug. A hug does not require specific reasons, either. Give one just to being giving one. Give one and hold the embrace until a connection on the heart level is made, and then hold it for as long as the moment allows.

Hugging, like smiling, offers many benefits to the giver and the receiver. Here are just a few examples of the benefits received in our relationships when we hug often and deeply:

➢ A hug satisfies our need for touch. Touch is the first sense that we acquire, and physical contact remains a necessity in our lives. Many people are touch deprived and people do not receive a daily hug. Nearly seventy-five percent of people desire more hugs. Hugs are essential to our well-being.

➢ Hugs increase the bond we have with our partner and they strengthen the relationship. The simple act of hugging keeps the relationship healthy and happy. Hugging bridges the gap between what happens in the bedroom and what happens in day-to-day living. Hugging maintains intimacy in a relationship.

➢ Hugs have been proven to be more important for a couple's happiness than sex. Hugging provides closeness and connection as well as acceptance. Hugging assists us in maintaining an emotional bond with our partner.

➢ Additionally, hugs increase empathy and understanding.

➢ Hugs Increase happiness.

➢ Hugs are great for our sex lives.

➢ Hugs teach us to give and receive.

And if those were not enough reasons to hug more deeply and frequently, here are some health benefits we receive from hugging:

➢ Hugging helps fight stress induced illness.

➢ Hugging boosts our immune system.

200

- ➢ Hugging reduces stress.
- ➢ Hugging increases Serotonin levels.
- ➢ Hugging balances out our nervous system.
- ➢ Hugs are anti-aging.
- ➢ Hugging protects against heart disease.
- ➢ Hugging relieves pain.
- ➢ Hugging assists us to move through depression.
- ➢ Hugging eases our fear of mortality.
- ➢ Hugging can help with insomnia and anxiety.
- ➢ Hugging decreases our food cravings.
- ➢ Hugs elevate our self-esteem.
- ➢ Hugging helps us relax on the physiological and psychological levels.

All these wonderful benefits of hugging, and those we saw with smiling, add up to this truth: When we authentically smile and hug often, we feel more loving and loveable. What greater tool can we have than one that gives and receives love? We serve our relationship, ourselves and our partner when we create a habit of deeply hugging and smiling from our heart throughout the day.

Have Fun

Fun is much more than having a good time. It is truly vital to our growth and learning. To elevate anything, we serve ourselves and our growth when we add fun.

For many of us, when our relationship became serious, we left behind the fun. For most of us, when we find ourselves in a difficult situation within the relationship, we get serious and leave fun out of the situation. We have been taught that a serious situation requires us to be serious which, for many of us, takes on a somber aspect. We move into areas that are somewhat dark and match our emotions to the situation we are facing.

When we become serious about a circumstance we face, the situation takes on a more serious feeling. When we add dark emotions like worry, upset, sadness, anger or fear to a dark situation, we will only add more darkness. Light is elusive; love is left out.

It is said that dark will never defeat darkness, only light can do that. Adding light pierces the darkness and illuminates our path to resolution and healing. Light allows all that is good to become known. The dark emotions tempt us to ignore or avoid a situation while light allows us to move through it, find answers and transform it into an opportunity to grow and learn.

We add light by expressing love, and fun allows us to do this more easily and effortlessly. Including love and fun lightens the darkness, and we engage instead of ignoring and avoiding. With love and fun, fear ebbs and soon clears from the path to solutions.

Many of us have settled into a comfortable existence in our relationships. We get settled because to try something new and make changes, requires us to be vulnerable. To many of us, vulnerability is perceived as weak and fearful, and we avoid it at all costs.

We can adjust our perception of vulnerability when we understand its power. Vulnerability can be an amazing resource in life situations. Vulnerability opens us to greater awareness and assists us to see beyond the negative details of the situation.

To add a visual perspective of this, consider, for a moment, a relationship as a dart board. There is a circle in the middle we call the bullseye, around the bullseye, we have a larger circle and outside of that is an even larger circle. The bullseye, where we set our aim in darts, is the smallest of the three circles. It is the goal we hope to achieve. This is where the prize can be found. The more darts we throw at the target, the more tired we become making it harder and harder to hit our goal.

In relationship, this inner circle represents our comfort zone. We find great comfort here, however, it is small and limiting. The more effort we put into reaching this comfort zone, the more difficult it becomes to find the comfort we seek. In fact, even when we do hit the bullseye, the comfort we find there is temporary at best. Comfort zones will shrink if we do nothing to expand them. How awesome would it be if we could enlarge the bullseye and make it easier to hit?

We enlarge our comfort zones by testing the boundaries of what we find comfortable. Before we explore ways to expand our comfort zones, I want to share an example of how comfort zones shrink.

Our example comes from a story of a woman who was found living in a closet of her home. The beginning of her story was like most of ours. She had a job she loved. She did her shopping at the local grocery and department stores. She had friends who she met for dinner on occasion. Her home was beautiful and around the home was a yard where she enjoyed gardening. She had a patio she used for relaxation. She was nestled into a life she found quite comfortable.

Her comfort was so pleasing to her, she never attempted to expand her experience of life. Her comfort zone began to shrink. She began to fear going to work. Instead of stepping through the fear, she gave in to it. She found a way to work from home; therefore, she had no need to face her fear. This was before the days of internet, so working from home was not as easy as it is today and many people including herself, considered her ability to work out of her house as a true gift. A delivery service brought her work each morning and picked up what she had done the day before.

Her fear began to expand beyond the workplace and soon, the grocery and department stores became fearful to her. Again, she gave into her fear and to avoid the pain of fear, she found a way to phone in her orders and have them delivered. It was not long before the people delivering her groceries, shopping and work were unsafe. All deliveries were then left on the front porch and she would retrieve them only after the delivery person left the property.

Somewhere along the way, her fear tightened its grip again and she could no longer attend dinners and functions with her friends or family. Her yard and garden became unsafe and even her house became unsettling for her. Her children found her living in the only safe place she could find - her closet.

204

While this is an extreme example, we all have comfort zones that shrink if we do not continually try new things. Each of us has personal comfort zones in our relationship. The routines we follow day in and day out are part of our comfort zones. The feelings we consider normal are part of our comfort zone.

When we fall into the pattern of collapsing onto the couch each evening, numbing out to the TV and then crawling into bed day in and day out, our comfort zone will shrink. This pattern may offer comfort when we first begin. Our partner may even settle into it with us, however, eventually, the comfort zone will shrink, and these practices will no longer offer comfort.

Fortunately, we have internal indicators that tell us when our comfort zone is shrinking. We may find it more difficult to get up and go to work. We may find our energy level drops to the point we do not go out in the evenings. We may suddenly not know how to communicate with our partner any longer. We may begin seeing our partner with judging eyes instead of appreciation. We may find that our bond with the couch and TV are stronger than our bond with our partner.

The busyness of life often becomes an excuse for not trying anything new. The stress of our lifestyle steps in with the threat to overwhelm. We tire of trying to expand our comfort zone. This inner circle, the bullseye, the comfort zone, closes in and the comfort is gone where once we had peace.

To open our comfort zone and allow it to grow, we must expand the perimeter. We do that by pushing into the second circle of the dart board I mentioned earlier that represents our relationship. This second circle represents the learning zone. This is where learning and growth happen. As we push out from our comfort zone, as we expand our experience in and of our relationship, we extend the boundaries of our comfort zone. This second circle is the key to our joy and happiness, however, even this circle is limited unless we expand it.

It is difficult to gather the strength and courage to press into the learning zone due to the outer circle that looms just beyond learning. Along the outer rim of the learning zone begins the outer most circle - fear. As human beings, it is our desire to avoid fear and this is the reason many of us choose to remain trapped where we are. Ultimately, when we settle for staying the same, our comfort zone begins to shrink.

As discouraging as this may sound, there is a key ingredient that expands the learning zone and pushes fear far away. This ingredient is FUN. Adding fun keeps fear at bay, expands the learning zone, allows us to travel deep into the second circle without fear and ultimately, expands our comfort zone. It is here we learn new things, try new experiences, and enjoy the process.

When something is fun, we step further into it. We are still vulnerable each time we stretch outside of our comfort zone, however, as we add fun, push fear away, openly embrace the vulnerability, the task is enjoyable instead of fearful. We are more open to consider, and experience change and new ideas.

We can bring fun into every situation and experience. The situation may be serious; our response to it does not have to be. The fun mentioned here is not about being silly and denying the situation. It is about giving seriousness a day off. We can take a serious situation, continue giving it the attention and respect it is due and have fun in seeking resolution or solution.

The routines and behaviors where we have settled can be a thing of the past when we seek options with fun. Even if the alternative option is reading a book about relationship tools with our partner, we can have fun in the process. Even if the option we choose is a walk in the woods, we can make it fun and the challenges we may face in walking instead of sitting on the couch, become easier to address. Adding fun to anything expands our ability and our desire. We can experience the expansion of our comfort zone with mindfulness and fun, and we can expand the things we allow into our experience.

We allow our relationship, and all things in life, to expand by adding fun. In the next section, we introduce Sacred Rituals that can be practiced with fun and love. And, it is in fun and love that we truly expand and elevate our relationship and life.

Create
Sacred Rituals

Elevate and Expand

Your Experience of Love

Sacred Rituals

The busyness of the world has built walls in most relationships. In the beginning of our relationship, we find tremendous amounts of time and energy for each other. As the newness of the relationship wears off, worldly needs take over again and we are back to the grind with our jobs, commitments to friends and family and any number of other time and energy consuming activities. The time we devote to elevating our relationship is the first place we begin to take the relationship and our partners for granted. The energy we devote to our relationship, partner and ourselves is a close second, or third, or somewhere further down the line of our priorities.

To elevate and expand the relationship, we must value the devoted time we have with our partner and expand the energy we spend on the relationship, our partner and ourselves. To continue building our relationship with our greatest ally and companion, our partner, we must elevate our relationship to the number one spot in our list of values and priorities. We must express love more fully in all we do.

While time does seem to be quite limited, recognition of our values and reorganization of our priorities are possible. With this recognition and reorganization, we find positive shifts in our energy as well.

I once saw a wonderful demonstration about time management. It began with a professor placing a large glass jar on a table. She then filled the jar with several large rocks until it could no longer receive another large rock. The professor asked the class, "Is this jar full?" to which the class unanimously answered "Yes". The professor then pulled a bag of gravel out and poured the gravel into the jar until no more gravel would fit. She again asked if the jar was full. Most of the class again answered "Yes." The professor revealed a jar of sand and poured that into the large jar until the jar could accept no more sand. Asking the question again the class reluctantly answered "Yes," once again. Finally, the professor brought out a jar of water and poured it into the jar until it could accept no more water.

The professor proceeded to tell the class that when we take care of our priorities first, there is time to take care of the other things. When we take care of the big things in our life, the small things can be accomplished within the gaps.

We often become invested in getting the small things done first, leaving no time or room to handle the big things. We become so exhausted keeping up with the minor details of life that we have no energy for those things of great importance.

When we cannot find time or energy for our partner and relationship, we are basically devaluing them and identifying the relationship as being a lower priority than the things that fill the day. Conversely, when we hold our relationship and our partner as our highest priority, we expand and elevate the relationship and all other things work out. In this reorganization, highest good, our greatest values, and our highest priorities are served.

By elevating our relationship, we realize that our spouse or significant other can be our greatest ally and partner in all we do. We find they are great support when we face issues at work. We find a companion to support us when family or friend issues arise. Whether it be in romance, work, general support or anything else, our partner is important to our success, just as we are to theirs.

Granted, most of our jobs take up tremendous amounts of time, so we must add value to the time we spend with our partners. Creating Sacred Rituals is a tool that will help.

The title of this section can be misleading, and clarification is needed before we begin. As we spoke of earlier, the words we use can often be mis-interpreted or carry several meanings. To insure understanding and clarity, let us define Sacred Rituals as they are intended in this text.

A definition of "Sacred Rituals," as far we are concerned, is simply the practices we use in our relationship that open opportunities to expand and elevate love and understanding.

Once we choose to practice these Sacred Rituals, we practice them often, and we do not allow the demands of a busy lifestyle to prevent us from the practice.

The word, "Sacred," is often attached to a religious meaning. For the purposes of this book, "Sacred" simply means, devoted exclusively to one service, and the service intended here is to more deeply expand and experience love.

The word "Ritual," means committing to a practice with intention. Someone striving to learn how to play a guitar, for instance, will practice often and may become a good player. When they commit to the practice, turn it into a non-negotiable part of their day, and include their heart in the practice, they create a ritual with intention. With this intentional ritual, they move beyond being a player and become a musician.

Rituals with the intention of expanding love elevate us from being in love to being an expression of love. We

211

move from waiting for love to come to us to being creators of love.

The practices presented here, or any practice used to elevate and expand love within the relationship, are important due to the infinite evolution we and our partners experience. Each day, we grow and change, and a devoted practice of these Sacred Rituals expands our awareness of the growth. The continued and frequent practice of these rituals give us a resource for infusing the relationship with authentic love throughout all growth we experience.

The sacred rituals presented here, and others, are intimate and personal. While the tools presented in this book can be adapted to every aspect of our lives, these Sacred Rituals are intended for use in the relationship.

As with the tools presented in this book, these Sacred Rituals are suggestions. Since we are all unique individuals, some adjustments may be required to create the perfect ritual for each relationship. We can choose to use them as written, we can adapt them to our own lifestyle, we can change them in any way we see fit or we can choose to create our own.

The key is to use Sacred Rituals in the relationship that offer opportunity to expand and elevate the connection with our partner. When we find and use practices that open awareness and communicate love and appreciation, we elevate and expand the relationship.

Vision Love

In the previous section, we addressed visioning our relationships and setting intentions. We now take visioning even deeper as we explore "Vision Love." While this practice is a beautiful tool, it is also a sacred ritual.

With all the chaotic situations we face in our lives and relationships these days, it is easy to become overcome with anger, sadness and anxiety. Stress sets in and if left unattended, these feelings increase, fear strengthens, and the well-being of the relationship is tested. Our physical health is even at risk.

The stress we feel comes from within. The power that any situation has over our feelings and emotions is based on the power we give to those situations. Nothing can stress us out unless we give it the okay to do so. Having said that, this does not mean we walk around like zombies and care nothing about what is happening in our relationship or the world. We can care deeply about circumstances in our lives and relationships and still have power over the stress that attempts to well up inside of us.

This first sacred ritual will certainly provide opportunity to relieve stress. When practiced without judgment and comparison to others, this practice will transform stressful situations into experiences of love and peace. As we "Vision Love," we expand and elevate love.

As mentioned in the earlier chapter about visioning, it is very important that we do not insert the word "for" between Vision and Love. We are not visioning for love.

When we vision "for" something, we see the lack of that thing, and it pushes what we desire further away from us. Visioning for something sometimes assists in calming our experience; however, most times it adds to the stress as we see the lack of that which we are visioning. To manifest our desires, we must Vision that thing, not "for" that thing.

To Vision Love, connect with your inner sacred space. Move to that place within your own being where you fully experience Love. See the love that already exists in your life. See and deepen the love you have for yourself. Embrace the love that resonates within.

Calm your heart and connect with your highest self, God, Universe, higher power, whatever that may be for you. Remember that this love is already within; you do not need to wait for it to arrive from an outside source, and it is not given because of your deeds or beliefs. It is not something you must earn; it is unconditional, it is already within and it is abundant.

The tendency is to seek love, or any other desire, outside of you. When you do this, you become reliant on someone else to provide love or you come to believe that certain circumstances must be in place before you can receive. You may even believe you must change so that you are deserving of love. Never forget that who you are as a beautiful essence, your truth, is all you ever need to be. Love resonates within you. Simply open your heart to experience it and embrace it.

The only change ever needed is not to become something else, rather it is to release the illusions and conditional thinking that prevent you from embracing your truth and love. Release anything that empowers the belief that you are less than or not good enough. Vision and embrace Love.

Once you embrace the love within, two things occur:

First, your need for the external love dissipates. It is not that love cannot be found outside of you, it is that your "need" fades. When need fades, you are not dependent on those external sources of love; you do not compromise your integrity, your truth. Your self-value and self-worth remain strong and you realize you do not need to earn love; it is already yours. When your need fades, you remain true to you and know that the love within is plentiful.

The second thing that occurs when you realize inner love always resonates throughout your life is that you more openly realize, understand and receive the love that truly is coming from others and circumstances outside of you. Once you embrace the love within, you open yourself to the love that does come from your partner. Until you recognize what you have within, your truth, you will never recognize what comes to us from others.

How awesome would it be to be embraced by unconditional love in every moment of life? Well you are.

The Vision Love Practice

Take a moment to settle your mind, begin a gentle rhythmic breathing pattern and allow your eyes to close. Focus only on the present moment. When you become fully present, all is well. Even if you have serious health concerns, financial worries, difficulties with others, in this moment, when you tune into your breathing and calm your thoughts, all is truly well.

Embrace this truth and believe this truth. If you are having a difficult time believing that all is well, pretend for a moment that everything is well in the present moment. Anytime you want something, if you struggle with believing it is impossible, pretend that it is possible. When you can pretend something is possible, you make it so. If you can imagine it, it is absolutely possible.

Continue your rhythmic breathing, allow your mind to calm and feel peace. This is the internal love already discussed. Even if you only have a fleeting moment of this feeling, you are experiencing love. Feel it, embrace it and be grateful for it.

Now, turn your attention to something you can love about you. Embrace that, be grateful for that. Now, turn your attention to something else you can love about you. Feel it, embrace it and be grateful for it. It is important to stay present and to look within. Remember these are things you love about you. The things you love about others or the life you live come later. Right now, you are experiencing love within.

Feel it, embrace it and know this is your truth and know there is much more available when you open awareness to it and receive. Once again, hold that love in gratitude.

As you embrace gratitude for anything, you receive more that is worthy of gratitude. When you set your focus on one thing you love and hold it with gratitude, you become open to see something else you love and then another until the "feeling" of love resonates fully within.

As you continue this practice you will quickly fill your entire being with love, you will fill it so full that it spills out into the life you live through your expression into the world. When you are expressing authentic love out into the world, authentic love begins coming back to you in abundance.

Once you feel love, you can Vision Love. You are not visioning for love as that will put your focus on the lack of love. Vision love. With eyes closed, mentally and emotionally, move into the experience of love. In your vision, feel the abundance of love that fills you and the world around you.

See your life as love fills every moment you experience. See love everywhere present. See life as the world responds with an abundance of authentic love. Feel it within you and around you. Know what this feels like.

Now, see your relationship overflowing with love. See the flow of love between you and your partner. See love infused in every action and word that are shared in the relationship. See the relationship itself as pure love.

What sights come to mind when love is your experience? What sounds do you here when love resonates within and around you? What other feelings expand as you experience love? How does it show up for you? How do you express it more fully? How do you receive it from your partner? How do you give it to your partner? How do you love you?

Experience this with no conditions or expectations. Authentic love is unconditional; it is already within and it also comes to us from everything around us. Simply ask the questions and allow the answers to appear, celebrate them and embrace Love. Take your time with this as the experience itself will elevate the love you feel in your life.

If you feel blocked in any way, ask, "What can I release that will open me to this authentic love? Where have I withheld love that I can now express love?"

Feel, see and hear love around you. Vision this as if it is done. Vision your relationship embraced by love. Vision your relationship expressing unconditional and abundant love. See you and your partner in this ever-deepening love. See the love you express to them and feel the love you receive.

As the vision takes shape, tune into the feelings that you feel in your heart. Know the feelings associated with a loving life. Know the feelings you experience by being a loving and loveable person. Really anchor in the feelings you experience in this vision.

Spend time visioning love. Enjoy the experience. Have fun with the vision.

As you come to completion with your vision and truly feel love everywhere present, speak, silently or aloud, a heartfelt YES to your vision. Claim it as your truth and believe it is already made manifest in your relationship. It is the belief that creates the reality.

As you do this for the first time, some of your vision may seem impossible. Allow that perception to fade away. If you can imagine it, when you vision it, it is possible. Everything is possible when you believe and commit to the steps of your vision.

When doubt comes into your mind about your experienced in your vision, remember, that you are on a journey. Move into your vision again and feel. Open your awareness to life and feel the feelings of your vision embracing you in the present moment.

When you hold true to your vision and you feel love everywhere present, the journey you take expands and elevates love within and throughout your relationship and life. Celebrate and hold in gratitude what you just experienced and each step along your journey.

Visioning Love does not require participation from your partner. Obviously, if they are willing to participate, create a time when you both can experience this and Vision Love in your own ways. When complete, you can share your experience with each other or remain silent.

Vision Love often. Allow your vision to expand, and as you do, the love in your relationship and life expands as well.

Create Romance

Just as our experience of love needs to be re-kindled, so does the romance in our relationship. We often fall into a routine that serves only to pay the bills, provide food and shelter, and survive life. We are often so tired at the end of our day, we do not have the energy to ignite the spark of romance except on those few special occasions.

Romance is critical to the ongoing growth of love and excitement in the relationship. Now, do not get confused here: romance does not equal sex. It can certainly include sex; however, romance is much more complex than the occasional physical experience of each other.

Romance carries several meanings, many of which are described in stories, medieval tales and heroic adventures. For our purposes, romance is defined as emotional attraction, an aura which deeply embraces the relationship, an adventure of love and/or an expression of love. Romance empowers the tool mentioned earlier about love being a verb. Romance puts Love in action.

By applying the tools of this book to our relationship, our partner, and ourselves, we plant the seeds of love and understanding; however, for those seeds to grow, we must nurture those seeds. Elevating romance in our relationships provides the much needed nourishment that invites love to grow and enrich.

Romance can be experienced and expressed in many ways. The most obvious are romantic dates and these usually come around special events such as anniversaries, birthdays and holidays. While these anniversary, birthday or holiday dates can certainly elevate the romance of the relationship, why limit romantic dates to those special occasions? What would happen if we created romantic events or atmospheres in addition to the "special occasions"?

Romance is available always. There is no limit to how romance is expressed other than the limits we put in place with our own minds. Opening awareness to the possibility of romance throughout our relationship, in all areas of our relationship, we grow love and romance in all we do.

Romance does not require going on dates. In fact, romance does not require going anywhere. The level of romance in our relationship is not dependent on how much money we throw its way. In fact, we can grow the romance in the relationship without spending one cent.

We create romance and nurture it by opening awareness to it and embracing each moment as an opportunity to elevate it. Romance is not difficult, and it does not need to be a chore. It does not require great planning or extravagant actions. As wonderful as those romantic evenings can be, romance can be found in the simplest of moments.

Here are some ideas that may get the creative juices flowing as you consider how to elevate romance in your relationship:

> At your next meal, even if it is pizza or burgers, add a candle to the table. Dim the lights and put on some music that allows you and your partner to relax into each other's company. Set the stresses of the day aside for a moment and talk to each other.

221

➢ Go outside and look to the heavens together. Take in the beauty of the night sky. Enjoy a nature walk with your partner.
➢ Flirt with each other. As you walk through a store, flirt, tease, have fun with one another.
➢ Turn the lights down low, turn on some music you both enjoy and dance a slow dance while holding each other in a loving embrace.

There are many ways to create more romance in your relationship. Consider how you can transform activities you already do into romantic experiences. Add new activities if you wish. Remember to leave the comparisons out of the mix; what is romantic to you may not be considered romantic by your friends and family. You are not creating romance with them. This is between you and your partner. There are no limits, no right way to do it or wrong way. Follow your heart.

Create Sacred Time Together

This sacred ritual aligns beautifully with the previous one, Create Romance. With "Create Sacred Time Together," we are invited to turn off the routines we so easily participate in each day. Turning our focus from the TV to our partner, we can experience greater understanding and appreciation for them.

The entire universe is constantly expanding; so are we and so is our partner. When we allow life to slip by without tuning in, we miss the evolution of our partner and it will seem as if we have grown apart. Creating sacred time together allows us to open our awareness to our partner's evolution and our attention tells them we care. When we are aware of their evolution, we can support them, and our love is given the opportunity to expand.

This sacred ritual is a daily commitment to each other. "Create Sacred Time Together" is much more than being in the same vicinity with our partner as we go through the motions of daily life. This is one on one time where we are devoted to and focused on each other. Even if it is just 15 minutes a day, we can take time to focus on each other without the distractions of the TV, phones, busyness. This is time we tune in to each other.

Fill this time with anything that allows you to connect more deeply with your partner. Some ideas to consider:

➤ Have a conversation about your day, about something you would like to do together, talk about

223

likes, dislikes. Have this conversation from the heart. Explore beyond the surface level conversation most of us have.

➢ Use this time to Vision Love.
➢ You can use this time to create a romantic atmosphere.
➢ Spend this time sitting in silence, holding hands, cuddling. Simply share love, express love and receive love.
➢ Sit silently looking deeply into each other's eyes.

Remember, this part of the sacred ritual is a daily practice. Find ways to keep this exciting, loving and even fun. Consider 15 minutes each day to begin and totally focus on each other. If you cannot do 15 minutes, try 10. If this is difficult, give 5 minutes a try and allow the time to expand as you begin to experience the benefit of this focused time together.

The next part of the sacred ritual is designed to encourage you to take time each week where you and your partner go out and do something together, just the two of you. Do something that is not part of your normal routine.

A list of possible ways to practice this include:

➢ Date Night. This is always a fun option. If a movie is your choice, make time afterwards to chat and be together, focused on each other. Talk about your experience of the movie. Talk about anything that allows you to learn more about each other. Make the heart connection between you and your partner a higher priority than the movie. If a dinner date is more appealing, allow the conversation and experience of each

224

other to be a higher priority than the food you eat; and leave your phones in the car or better yet, at home.

➢ Take walks, holding hands, enjoying each other's company.

➢ Begin a Yoga class together, or some other sort of exercise. Allow time after the activity to connect on the heart level and lovingly support each other and celebrate together each new milestone.

➢ Take walks in nature and go for a hike where you pack a picnic lunch. Get off the beaten path and relax together as you enjoy lunch, the surroundings and most importantly, each other.

➢ Take your picnic to a lakeshore or beach if you have one nearby.

➢ Take a camping trip together.

➢ Bike riding, motorcycling, exercising, golf and other sports activities are all activities couples sometimes enjoy together. Again, be sure the experience of each other holds more importance than the activity.

➢ Take a class together that broadens your mind or a cooking class or maybe pottery. Find one that agrees with you both. The beauty of taking a class together is that the experience can easily continue for years and the more you do it, the more the experience of each other evolves.

➢ Candle Lit Baths, massages, Hot Tubs, Saunas are incredibly intimate ways to create sacred time together.

One couple I know took up skydiving together. They get excited every time they begin planning their next jump and make this focused time together. They enjoy the personal exhilaration of the jump itself then spend time with each other after the jump to celebrate and talk about their experience.

Another couple loves to do ziplines. Like the parachutists, they get to enjoy the personal journey of each zipline experience and then come together to share their experiences.

The options are limitless. The key to any of your options, though, is to make sure there is opportunity to connect more deeply with your partner. What you do is not as important as the quality time you have with each other away from the stress of daily life.

Make this fun and exciting. Make this practice something you can both look forward to each week. Mix it up too. Find several different things. Try new things that neither of you have ever done before. Take turns introducing each other to activities you may have enjoyed before on your own.

As you enjoy this sacred time together, allow the friendship between you and your partner to expand. Your partner can be the greatest friend you can ever have. If they are not in that position already, consider what it means to have your best friend by your side in all you do. If they are in that position, consider how you can expand the friendship beyond what it is now.

The friendship will support you in times when love may seem distant. The friendship helps to keep fun available in every situation. When your romantic partner is also your best friend, you empower your romantic life to stay strong through good times and bad.

"Create Sacred Time Together," expand the friendship and watch your relationship blossom and grow; experience deeper love as it ignites with renewed vigor.

See Them for the First Time, Again

Do you ever feel like the magic has left the relationship? You know, in the beginning every time you laid eyes on your partner, there was a flutter. Their smile gave you goose bumps, and you felt so amazingly special when they looked at you. You just couldn't wait until the next time you got to see them. The time together seemed magical. Then one day you turned around and something just seemed to be missing and things were not the same as they were when you first met? Even if the love is still there, is the spark? The romance? The tingles of joy each time you look at them?

This sacred ritual is one that is truly a gift to every couple. It has healing powers and will rekindle embers of love that may have been dormant for years. For the couples who still experience each other's love each day, this sacred ritual will deepen that love and expand it even further.

The sacred ritual is, "See Them for the First Time, Again," and it may be the most important practice you can begin in your relationship. This practice will fuel that roaring fire that was once the center piece of your relationship.

If you can get your partner to participate in this exercise, excellent. You will need to schedule thirty minutes of uninterrupted time for the full experience. If you think thirty-minutes too long, commit to twenty minutes. If your partner will not participate, do not worry, you can adjust this practice and receive many gifts, as well.

Let's start with the scenario where your partner will participate.

Create an atmosphere of romance. If you play music, have it very low as background music. Remove all distractions. Turn off phones, turn off computers and TVs, let the kids spend the night with friends, put the pets in another room, wait until after the process to begin the dishwasher - you get the picture.

The room can be very bright or romantically lit with candles or soft lighting. The only requirement for lighting is there must be enough light to easily see your partner's eyes and vice versa. Make sure your eyes are not in the shadows.

Sit facing each other; as close together as possible without touching. You may use chairs, the floor, the bed, a bench - anywhere you can sit comfortably for the entire exercise is fine. Again, the key is to be as close to each other as possible without touching.

Be sure there is nothing between the two of you. You will sit fully facing each other with your entire body. Only cross your legs if you are in lotus position on the floor and allow your hands to rest gently in your lap.

This sacred ritual is practiced in complete silence, other than music if you so choose; no verbal communications at all. Silently look deeply into each other's eyes. Notice the sparkle in their eyes. See the flecks of different colors there. Spend time here as if you are memorizing what you see. Once you have journeyed into the beauty of their eyes, look even deeper. Peer into their pupils and then see deep beyond the surface. See the light of their heart, their soul, their love, their authentic self. Spend time here renewing what you fell in love with in the first place and see if you can discover something new in them.

See them as if you are seeing them for the first time. See them as if you are looking directly into their essence; that perfect part of them, their truth. Maintain eye contact and silence for the duration of this exercise. See them with renewed interest and again, see them as if you are seeing them for the first time and feel the feelings you had that initially brought you together.

As you experience each other's hearts, express the deep love and appreciation you have for them. Send them non-verbal messages of gratitude and peace and well-being. Express all that you desire to say to them that elevates love.

Receive the love and gratitude they send to you. Be open to experience the expressions of their heart. Embrace the feelings of abundant love that rise within you. Memorize these feelings.

This sacred ritual is about being fully present; mindfully in the moment. Do not go into this exercise with any expectations about what this may be or where it may lead. Simply allow the connection and embrace the feelings.

This is an extremely intimate process and the temptation to reach out for physical contact before completing the allotted time is often strong. Give yourself and your partner the full gift of this process and follow through with the full thirty-minute exercise before touching.

At the end of your time, do what feels right. You may want to take a moment with or without your partner to silently process what you just experienced and when you are able, talk about your experience. You may want to embrace your partner. Honor your experience in ways that express your feelings and love.

Do this for a minimum of 30 minutes. If at some point during this process you realize you cannot make it the full thirty minutes, be grateful for what you did and do the exercise again soon. Make this a regular experience and you will be amazed at the results.

If your partner is unwilling to participate, you can still experience this sacred ritual. Before you begin, consider these questions.

Did you explain the process and ask them to join you? Many people assume they know what their partner is willing or unwilling to do and act accordingly. Leave assumption out of it and simply ask your partner to join you in this ritual.

Did your partner refuse because of the timing? Was it going to interfere with something they had planned? Do not throw this sacred ritual away. Simply ask if you both can agree on a time and schedule it.

Was the process too long for them to commit? Ask if they will participate in a shortened version of it. You can still realize great benefits in the shortened version, thirty-minutes just allows you to go deeper into the experience. Once they participate in a ten-minute version, they may be willing to do fifteen minutes or twenty or even thirty.

Now, if you have considered these questions and your partner is just not willing to participate, you can still experience this on the individual level. Do not go into judgment about them; understand they may have underlying issues that cause them to avoid this level of intimacy. Also know that they may not be ready to consider this practice now but may be willing to later.

For you to participate on your own, you must first forgive your partner's unwillingness. Allow any negativity to fade away and open your heart to the person you love.

With a clear mind and open heart, begin a gentle rhythmic breathing pattern. Silence your mind and simply watch your partner. Observe them doing whatever they are doing with an open heart. Study their profile while they watch TV. Tune into their reactions as they read a book. Notice how their body moves when they are exercising or walking the dog. Simply find a way to see the wonder of them.

Once you feel the love for what you can see with your physical eyes, look deeper. Study their heart, their soul, see their authentic truth. When you look beyond their surface, you will begin to feel a shift. Your awareness of their true self and the growing love you have for them will expand.

As you see your partner with expanded love, you will express love more deeply, and you will interact with them more peacefully and lovingly. These expressions and actions will be felt by your partner and could very well lead to more loving actions and expressions from them as well.

Make this sacred ritual a regular practice. The more you look within your partner's heart, the more connection to them you will feel. As your connection to their true self expands, so does love.

The Heart Dance

I learned this dance more than 25 years ago, and it was introduced to me as the Sufi Dance. Over the years it has evolved somewhat, so I now call it the Heart Dance because it truly is a dance where you and your partner will connect on the heart level.

This dance remains to be the only dance I know. I never learned how to dance any of the popular dances and on the rare occasion I did attempt to learn some steps, I was never considered light on my feet. Dancing is just not my thing, so I do not put any effort into any other dance. I tell you this because this dance has no steps. I only learned it because of the heart connection it offered.

If you or your partner, like me, do not dance, no worries, you can do this one beautifully because the focus, attention and intention is on each other's hearts, not the steps.

The Heart Dance Process:

First, set the atmosphere. Dim the lights but keep enough light that you can see into each other's eyes without shadows.

For this sacred ritual, music playing very softly in the background is beneficial, however, not mandatory. Keep the music soft and relaxing - nothing that will distract your attention or disrupt the mood.

232

The dance is done in silence with no verbal communications.

Stand face to face with your partner.

Have them put their right hand on your heart and you place your right hand on their heart. With your left hand, cover their right hand as it covers your heart and have them do the same.

Once your hands are in position, move closer together. Feel your body connecting fully with your partner's.

Look deeply into each other's eyes and express love. Express gratitude. Express kindness.

Again, this dance is done with no verbal communications, so all expressions are done through your eyes.

Begin to sway together slightly and allow the energy of the moment to dictate your movements. If you choose to take a step, do so. Know that it is perfect to stay where you are as you sway back and forth together.

Send loving thoughts. Send thoughts of peace and kindness. Express your compassion and gratitude for them. Send your heart to theirs. As you send this beautiful energy, realize how deep your love for your partner goes. Allow it to deepen, to grow, to expand and to fill you, them and the space around you both. Feel a loving embrace holding the two of you.

Receive the expressions of love coming from your partner. Feel the gratitude, kindness and peace they express to you.

Allow the music to move you. Allow the love to move you. Again, there are no required steps in the dance, just be moved.

Continue this dance for as long as it takes to really feel their heart, to make that heart connection. Once you feel it, continue for as long as you desire. Just as with "See Them for the First Time Again," go into this with no expectations other than the love and compassion you want to express.

In this Heart Dance, your primary intention is to send love and feel love expand within you. Hold no expectations for what your partner should feel or receive. Simply enjoy the closeness of the dance, send pure, loving energy and thoughts, and be open to whatever comes.

As with each of the sacred rituals, practice often. The more you practice, the deeper you connect on the heart level with you partner.

Summary

Relationships add texture to our lives. They add width and depth, longevity and soaring heights. Relationships allow us to fulfill our purpose as humans and that is giving and receiving love. Relationships can add light to your day and they can ignite places within you that you never knew existed. Relationships are powerful and provide so many more benefits than I can mention here.

Relationships can also be the opposite of all of these. It is truly our choice how to experience relationships.

It is important to remember that a relationship needs attention. Some relationships seem to cruise along easily and effortlessly. Some travel a rough road. The ones that seem easy are sometimes the ones that get taken for granted. The ones that seem to be a struggle often are the ones that become the strongest.

Now, this does not mean to go and create chaos in a smooth and easy relationship. It simply means to honor your relationship with attention and intention. If it is a struggle, you must not become discouraged. You can find gratitude for

235

what is working and express love over it all. Either way, easy or difficult, you must do the work, and the work can be fun.

You are unique. Your partner is unique. There is no one else in the world with your DNA, and no one else in the world with your partner's DNA. This makes it absolutely impossible for your relationship to be like anyone else's. You have the opportunity and the power to create your own perfect relationship. You can seek the ways things work best for you and your partner, and you can release the things that do not.

There are many teachers, coaches, churches, societies, friends and people you may run into during your day who will tell you how your relationship should be. Knowing that you are unique, and your partner is unique, you can embrace the truth that your relationship is unique. You can give yourself, your partner, and your relationship a break from the "rules" of relationships and create your own guidelines and agreements. You can create understandings that work for the both of you.

The answers you seek to elevate your relationship are found within, not out in the world. If the world knew the answer to great relationships, the "stay together" rate would out-weigh the divorce rate. While the experts may have wonderful ideas, those ideas must be used as a consideration, not a rule. You can consider the advice of experts long enough to decide if their advice works for you or not. If not, let it go.

This book is not a rule book for relationships. It is not even a guide book. It is simply written to offer ideas on where you can start turning things around to elevate love or lovingly expand things in your relationship that already serve highest good.

The tools and sacred rituals presented here must be used if you want them to assist you in elevating and expanding the love and experience of your relationship. Like a tool box full of carpenter's tools, if you do not pull the tools out, plug them in and get busy, they will not work, and you will build nothing. The tools that go unused will simply gather dust until the time that you can no longer recognize them for what they are. I can teach them to you, but you must choose to use them.

Pull these tools out and use them every day. Pick one each day that holds meaning for you and put it into practice. Give them a try as written and then, if needed, tweak them to better fit your needs.

As you discover a tool that serves a current need, write the tool name on a card and post it to your mirror, your computer or any place you will see it several times a day. This is an excellent reminder to use the tool.

Using these tools with love for you and your partner will elevate your experience of love and understanding.

As loving and powerful as these tools can be, they can also be used as weapons. Do not fall into the trap of starting tool wars. This occurs most frequently when both individuals in the relationship read and study the tools. In the middle of an argument, one may call out, "Choose to Be Happy Rather Than Right," or when one partner is critiquing the other, the one being critiqued may call out, "Leave Your Judgments by the Curb."

Arguments and other heated moments are not the time to bring up a tool suggestion. Step back, cool off and let the dust settle. Once peace is the presiding emotion, come together and then discuss the tools and how they can serve to elevate love. These tools are not designed to be weapons.

237

They are designed to be loving resources that will allow you to enrich your relationship.

As mentioned many times in this book, we live very fast-paced lifestyles. The search for quick fixes and "once and done" experiences lead us to many unsuccessful experiences. Most of us hope that once we use one of these relationship tools, we will never have to use them again. I truly wish that were true; however, no lasting relationship will ever be built upon one action, one attempt or one consideration. Lasting relationships are achieved when both partners give love and add value consistently.

If you use these tools only once, you will experience some benefit, however, continued use of them will lovingly and greatly transform you and your experience of the relationship. Even if your partner never reads a word of this book, they too will experience transformation to some degree simply by the transformed expressions you give into the relationship.

Elevate your relationship with love and understanding. Release the behaviors and beliefs that do not serve highest good for you, the relationship or your partner. Embrace the behaviors that do serve to lift your experience of love.

You are worthy of experiencing a beautiful and loving relationship. You now have tools to assist you in manifesting a relationship as good and better than you imagine.

Love and Peace,

Kenny

About the Author

For more than 25 years, Kenny Brixey has journeyed a path to life meaning, centeredness, purpose; his essence. On this journey, Kenny discovered his life purpose of teaching, mentoring and coaching others to realize their own essence and incredible awesomeness.

Kenny creates and presents widely sought after personal and professional programs offering authentic growth and transformative learning experiences. His personal growth seminars, workshops and team events assist individuals and groups in discovering their own unique strengths, talents and gifts.

Kenny is the spiritual director for Divine Connection - Center for Spiritual Awareness - in Van Alstyne, Texas.

Kenny is the creator and host of "Life's Tool Box" talk radio show which airs Mondays on Empower Radio. www.empoweradio.com Each week, Kenny discusses empowering tools that assist the listeners in living an empowered and authentic life.

In all his work as an author, personal/professional coach, minister and experiential speaker, he focuses on creating unique opportunities for individuals, couples and groups to reach their full potential by realizing their own infinite greatness.

Other books by Kenny:

Discovering The Divine Within

Awakening Insights

No Excuses, No Limits; Just Results

(Available at Amazon.com)

Connect on line:

www.kennybrixey.com

https://www.facebook.com/AuthenticRelationships/

https://www.linkedin.com/in/kennybrixey/

https://twitter.com/KennyBrixey

https://www.youtube.com/kennybrixey

Listen to Life's Tool Box with Kenny Brixey:

www.empowerradio.com

18213349R00144

Made in the USA
Middletown, DE
29 November 2018